To Mar

With gratitude for
your encouragement
and support.

God Bless —

Joe

ENDORSEMENTS

For many years Joe Barnett's words have been, for me, a source of fresh inspiration.

Max Lucado
America's bestselling author of inspirational books.

With tempered counsel, Joe Barnett shines eternal wisdom right where it hurts, and gives perspective that delivers fresh hope and direction for these turbulent times. He's not afraid to tackle the tough questions, and offers healing and comfort through personal and shared experiences that resonate on a deep level. *6 Verses* is a book I'll read again and again.

Tamera Alexander
Bestselling author of *A Lasting Impression*

When the storms of life threaten, where can we safely grab hold and hang on? In *6 Verses that Can Change Your Life* Joe Barnett provides a dependable and inspirational survival manual. His insightful and scriptural guidance provides shelter in the storms.

Dr. Andrew K. Benton
President, Pepperdine University

I have been inspired by Joe Barnett's thoughtful writings for many years. They have been extremely helpful to me in my Christian journey. This latest book is meaningful to us all as we encounter the inevitable storms.

Jack Scott, Ph.D.
Chancellor, California Community Colleges
California State Senator, 2000-2008

How easy it is to forget that God is there in the storms of our lives. This book puts God in the midst of our daily struggles and victories.

Jack Pope
Chief Justice (Retired), Texas Supreme Court

Grab hold of this book's engaging contents. Chew each section slowly, thoughtfully, prayerfully. And be grateful, as I am, for the marvelous reminders from this seasoned minister's words that point us, with realism, narratives, and humor, back to the One who knows us even better than we know ourselves.

Virgil Fry, D.Min.

Executive Director, Lifeline Chaplaincy

6 VERSES
THAT CAN CHANGE
Your Life

CROSSLINK
PUBLISHING

JOE BARNETT

6 VERSES

THAT CAN CHANGE

Your Life

TRUST   PATIENCE

ASSURANCE   COURAGE

PEACE   JOY

For many years Joe Barnett's words have been,
for me, a source of fresh inspiration.
~ Max Lucado

6 Verses That Can Change Your Life

CrossLink Publishing
www.crosslink.org

ISBN 978-0-9826215-9-2

CONTENTS

SECTION ONE

Trust

*Trust in the Lord with all your heart; do
not depend on your own understanding.*
—Proverbs 3:5 NLT

SECTION TWO

Assurance

*… (He) is able to do immeasurably more
than all we ask or imagine …
—Ephesians 3:20*

SECTION THREE

Courage

*Be strong and courageous!
Do not be afraid or discouraged.
For the Lord your God is with you wherever you go.
—Joshua 1:9 NLT*

SECTION FOUR

Patience

Wait for the Lord;
be strong and take heart
and wait for the Lord.
—Psalm 27:14 NIV

SECTION FIVE

Peace

Let him have all your worries and cares,
for he is always thinking about you and
watching everything that concerns you.
—1 Peter 5:7 TLB

SECTION SIX

Joy

This is the day the Lord has made;
let us rejoice and be glad in it.
—Psalm 118:24

ACKNOWLEDGEMENTS

I don't think anyone can write a book alone. I know I can't. A warm thank you to a few of those who helped birth this book:

Arlington Heights church in Corpus Christi, Texas—You let me guinea pig you with this material while I was writing it. Most of you stayed awake. That couldn't have been easy. I loved the time I spent with you. You are the best.

My Pathway partners—Your support, encouragement and affirmation through the years has been priceless. Thanks for believing in me and sticking with me in all kinds of weather.

Fred and Jan Alexander—Thanks for keeping Pathway stuff humming when I'm in writing hibernation. From college roommates to the present, Fred, it's been a great trip. It has been an honor to ride the trails with you.

Allen Isbell—My Rock of Gibraltar. If Merriam-Webster ever comes up with a definition for unconditional, loyal-to-a-fault friendship your picture will be beside it.

Jerry and Judy Gallagher—You were the first ones I talked to about this book. You said "do it." From beginning to end, you've been there. Thank you.

Marvin Crossnoe—Appreciation for your computer advice is exceeded only by gratitude for your meaningful friendship. Special thanks to your entire CoNetrix staff for kindness and patience in hand-holding this greenhorn who was out of the room when they wired brains for technology.

Melanie Rigney—Your early evaluation sent me in the right direction. Special thanks to you for helping me get on target, and for making me look smarter than I am.

Rick Bates and Crosslink Publishing—Thanks for your diligence in shepherding this work through the publishing process. It's an honor to partner with you.

You, the reader—As John Cheever said: "I can't write without a reader. It's precisely like a kiss—you can't do it alone." Thank you for entrusting me with a slice of your valuable time. I'll do my best to be a good steward of it.

Most of all, to my Lord—Thank you for letting me have a small part in your big work.

FOREWORD

Life is a spiritual journey.

Yet, we humans are bound by, and usually obsessed with, overwhelmingly mundane physical tasks and diversions. And more often than we would like, with simply trying to survive being battered by cruel storms.

But at our fingertips is a God who cares about, indeed incarnates, our limited physical world with limitless spiritual resources. Readers of this book are lovingly invited into a serious, fanciful chat about such soulful matters with skillful writer Joe Barnett.

At times we are convicted by the book's tenderness; at times we laugh aloud with its personal humor. And most of all, we are gently urged to tap the lushness of biblical narratives and focus verses.

Joe invites us into his own Christian worldview, a worldview being shaped as a profound student of God's Word and as a survivor of multiple difficult personal storms. This book never calls us to deny the pains we experience in the middle of losses. Joe rightfully urges us to acknowledge to God and to fellow travelers the reality of feeling deep sorrow.

Yet, the message comes through loud and clear: life storms do not have the final word. God offers us, in beautiful, clear ways, hope that can only come from a higher, loving Source.

Joe focuses on six verses that become the springboard for his invitation to consider our spiritual trek anew. Like a good friend sharing deep conversation over coffee, Joe's reflections serve as invitational dialogues with him, and more importantly, with the person looking back at me in the mirror.

We are invited, personally or with a trusted group, to pull back from overbooked schedules in order to relish the richness of practical theology. We are living "in the meantime," and we need God's hand in ours.

The six topics addressed are: trust, assurance, courage, patience, peace, and joy. Who of us, regardless of where we are spiritually, owns an overabundance of these valued commodities?

In our world of consumer-driven, success-oriented trappings, spiritual starvation runs rampant. Emptiness of the soul can only be filled by turning, again and again, to God's inexhaustible resources. Resources not just for survival, but for meaning and purpose beyond each storm's chaotic aftermath.

So I invite you to grab hold of this book's engaging contents. Chew each section slowly, thoughtfully, prayerfully. Use each section's summary resolutions as helpful checkpoints. Take the individual and group curriculum's guiding questions as an invitation to learn deeper appreciation for God's timing, God's counsel, God's love.

And be grateful, as I am, for the marvelous reminders from this seasoned minister's words that point us, with realism, narratives, and humor, back to the One who knows us even better than we know ourselves.

Virgil Fry, D.Min.
Executive Director
Lifeline Chaplaincy

LET'S GET STARTED

Meteorologists don't control the weather, only report it, and give precautionary recommendations when it turns nasty. Hearing the advice won't stop storms, but heeding it may save your life.

Likewise, hearing God's advice won't stop life's storms, but heeding it will assure survival.

> *Everyone who hears these words of mine and puts them into practice is like a sensible man who builds his house on the rock. Down came the rain and up came the floods, while the winds blew and roared upon that house—and it did not fall … (Matthew 7:24-25 PHILLIPS).*

The book you are holding is a selection of his words—a Survival Guide—packed in 6 verses. From these verses I have harvested the sections of this book …

Trust   Assurance   Courage   Patience   Peace   Joy

My prayer is that when storms litter your landscape—storms that dash your dreams, crush your hopes, and threaten your faith—you will find the shelter you need in these words.

—Joe Barnett

SECTION ONE

TRUST

*Trust in the Lord with all your heart; do
not depend on your own understanding.*
—PROVERBS 3:5 NLT

Without warning, a furious storm came up on the lake, so that the waves swept over the boat. But Jesus was sleeping. The disciples went and woke him, saying, "Lord, save us! We're going to drown!" ... he got up and rebuked the winds and the waves, and it was completely calm (Matthew 8:24-26).

T he wind is blowing harder than you ever remember. Through a rain-spattered window you see the trees bending until their branches kiss the ground.

An ear-splitting thunderclap puts every nerve in your body on edge. The computer screen flickers and goes blank. The TV fades to black with an ominous pop. The electric clock blinks ... 0:00 ... 0:00 ... 0:00. It's dark as a cave. You stare into the darkness, hoping your eyes will adjust, hoping the electricity will come back on. They don't. It doesn't.

You never realize how much you depend on light until you're without it, or how much you depend on God until all else fails.

It's not easy to trust the Lord in a world gone haywire, a world where storms seem to be winning. But it's the best thing you can do, because no one knows how to handle a storm like he does: *"He got up and rebuked the winds and the waves, and it was completely calm."*

Trust in the Lord with all your heart (Proverbs 3:5).

1

1628 9TH STREET

On Monday night, May 11, 1970, an F5 tornado sliced a chunk out of Lubbock, Texas. Its half-mile wide, eight-mile-long temper tantrum killed 26 people, injured 1500, destroyed 1,040 homes, damaged another 8,876, smashed more than 10,000 cars, and demolished 119 airplanes. It racked up the largest dollar damage of any tornado in U.S. history up to that time.

A charming little neighborhood of modest houses and neatly manicured lawns west of downtown was reduced to a wasteland of splintered trees and naked concrete foundations in a matter of minutes.

It was here, at 1628 9th Street, that Gus Niblack had built a small frame house for his new bride six decades earlier. They had lived here ever since. Gus was now 87; his wife Mary 82.

At first light Harvie Pruitt, Mary's nephew, started zigzagging through the tangle of debris-filled streets to check on the elderly couple. The scene was chilling, and he became increasingly apprehensive about the outcome of his mission. As Harvie turned onto 9th Street from Avenue Q his heart sank. Every house on the block was gone!

Except one!

Gus's and Mary's little home stood untouched, not a shingle missing.

Harvie knocked and shouted until his knuckles were bruised and his throat was raw. Finally, a disheveled half-asleep old man opened the door. Gus and Mary had slept right through the worst storm in the city's history.

Gus worked at Western Windmill his entire adult life. Never made much money. Never owned an automobile; walked to his job every day. I could tell you a lot about Gus—I knew him well—but this sentence tells you all you need to know: *Trust in the Lord with all your heart.*

That was Gus's mantra. His financial resources were meager, but many a millionaire would give all he has for the peace of this good man's trust-filled heart.

Was Gus singled out by God that night for favorable treatment? I don't know that he was. Or that he wasn't. But I do know this—if his little house had been flattened, his faith wouldn't have faltered. The needle would have held steady: *Trust in the Lord with all your heart.*

Storms are unavoidable. We don't call the shots that map the weather. When a hurricane makes landfall, an earthquake rearranges the furniture, or a tornado hurls bullet-speed shards of glass, we are at the mercy of nature.

We are equally helpless when personal storms waylay us. Your adversities are custom made—they have your name on them.

> The biopsy is positive.
> Your son is in the ER.
> The company is downsizing.
> The divorce is final.

When these storms strike there is no place to hide. You are fortunate indeed if you—like Gus—can trust in the Lord with all your heart.

He needed a break. It had been a long day—non-stop teaching and healing. *"Let's go over to the other side of the lake,"* Jesus said to his disciples (Luke 8:22). So off they went.

Before you could say "looks like rain" they were being pounded by an ill-tempered squall. And Jesus? He was catching some z's. While he snoozed, the disciples stewed. How could he sleep while they strangled on sea water? But they learned that if you get caught in a storm it's good to have Jesus in your boat.

"Help us!" they shouted.

"Be still!" he ordered.

And the storm stopped.

You may be in a teeth-rattling storm of your own right now. The water is rough, and deep, and cold. What Jesus did for them he can do for you.

That lesson on the lake rubbed off on Peter. Seventeen years later he was in jail in Jerusalem, set to be sentenced by blood-thirsty Herod Agrippa as soon as the sun came up. A death sentence was almost certain. Tonight was likely his last on earth. What did he do? He slept. (Acts 12:6).

That's what Gus Niblack did at 1618 9ᵗʰ Street the night the tornado trashed his neighborhood—he slept.

Can you have that kind of calm? Yes, you can—if you're in the right boat, with the right person.

Trust in the Lord with all your heart.

2

A MIXED BAG

Woody Allen allegedly said that he would find it easier to be a believer if God would deposit a large sum of money in his name in a Swiss bank account.

Woody sounds like Jacob.

Jacob was the favorite son of a conniving mom who home-schooled him. Her curriculum consisted of courses in Manipulation, Deceit, and Sleaze.

Give Jacob this, he was a crackerjack student: he mastered those courses. He cheated his brother and lied to his dad without blinking an eye. So trying to con God wasn't a stretch for him.

Listen in on his pitch:

> *If God will be with me and will watch over me...and will give me food to eat and clothes to wear...then the Lord will be my God...and of all that you give me I will give you a tenth (Genesis 28:20-22).*

There you go. Commitment with strings attached. The fine print is filled with *ifs*:

> *If* God will be with me,
> *If* God will watch over me,
> *If* God will give me food to eat,
> *If* God will give me clothes to wear …
> *Then* he will be my God.

"And ... ahem ... it's a good deal for you, God. Sign the contract and here's what you'll get out of it: I'll give you back a tenth of everything you give me!"

How could God refuse a deal like that?

> Protect me.
> Provide for me.
> Prosper me.
> Then you get me! Well, 10% of me.

Meet my terms. Measure up to my expectations. Justify my faith. Earn my trust. If you want me, that's the price.

Trust the Giver, Not the Gifts

Do you have a "Jacob's List"—requirements God must meet to gain your trust? If he met each of those conditions—like crossing items off of your grocery list as you drop them into the cart—would that do the trick? Cause you to trust him?

No it wouldn't. God isn't a cosmic gift-bringing grandparent: someone you're glad to see, not because of his presence, but because of his presents. You never know if you trust the Giver until you are deprived of the gifts. Never really know if you trust him until your dreams die—until you feel the pain of failure, hurt, loss.

Jacob's prayer gave God his marching orders: insisted that he deliver; dictated the terms. Trust doesn't lay down the terms. It lays down the need—then accepts the answer he sends, whatever it may be.

A prayer of trust runs something like this: "You are God; I'm not. You know what is best; I don't. I haven't come to you to tell you what to do; I have come to you to ask you to do what is best. I don't know what you will do, but I know it will be the right thing."

Don't entrust God with a problem if you're going to snatch it back when he doesn't handle it the way you want him to—or as quickly as you want him to. Trust the Giver, not the gifts.

A Mixed Bag

Have I painted a picture of trust that seems beyond your reach? If you are ready to throw up your hands and quit reading, don't. God won't scratch your name off the roll because you don't get an "A+" in trust this semester. Trust doesn't arrive full-grown. It grows inch-by-inch, year-by-year, frequently diluted by a pinch of uncertainty. Belief mixed with unbelief.

Here's a story that illustrates that mix.

One day Jesus took the "A" team—Peter, James and John—on a mountain hike. Something happened at the top of the mountain that the PJ&J trio would remember for the rest of their lives: Jesus' face began to glow, his clothes became eye-watering bright, and long-gone Moses and Elijah showed up and started talking with him. Peter, James and John were scared speechless. (Well, almost ... you know Peter.)

Meanwhile, down in the valley the "B" team wasn't playing well. A man had brought his seizure-suffering son for them to heal. They tried, but couldn't. When Jesus came down from the mountain the distressed dad was there to meet him: *"I asked your disciples to drive out the spirit, but they couldn't,"* he said.

While they were talking the little fellow fell into a fit—wallowing on the ground and foaming at the mouth; then becoming rigid as a corpse.

"How long has he been like this?" Jesus asked.

"All his life," said his father. "If you can do anything, take pity on us and help us."

"Everything is possible for him who believes," Jesus replied.

At that the man spit out as honest a confession as you'll ever hear: *"I do believe; help me overcome my unbelief!" (Mark 9:24).*

There's the mix—belief and unbelief in the same person. This isn't one person saying, *"I believe"* and a different person saying, *"help me overcome my unbelief!"* It's the same person saying both: belief and unbelief, saint and skeptic, living in the same skin.

"I believe"—there's the saint!

"Help me overcome my unbelief"—there's the skeptic!

Maybe you're struggling with the same mix. You believe, but not completely. You trust, but not totally.

A leper once said to Jesus, "If you *will,* you can make me clean" (Mark 1:40 RSV).

The best this father could manage was, "If you *can,* help us."

To the leper Jesus said, *"I will."*

To this father he said, *"I can."*

Depending on where you are, Jesus says *"I will"* or *"I can."*

Trust in the Lord with all your heart.

3

EASTER IS COMING

In 1974 Richard Nixon resigned as President of the United States rather than face impeachment.

Gerald Ford had been serving as nonelected Vice President for nine months, replacing Spiro Agnew. Now he became nonelected President, replacing Richard Nixon.

The country was in chaos. The pressure was enormous, and President Ford's wife Betty was quietly coming unhinged. One month after the swearing in she was diagnosed with breast cancer. Four years later she entered therapy for alcohol and prescription drug addiction.

President Ford had memorized the King James Version of Proverbs 3:5-6 as a boy: *"Trust in the Lord with all thine heart; and lean not unto thine own understanding. In all thy ways acknowledge Him and He shall direct thy paths."* These words became the guiding star for the President and First Lady.

"There are periods in life when we realize more than ever our life is not totally in our control," Betty said. "I have always looked to God … It provides a sense that no matter what happens, you will be okay, that you will ultimately survive any crisis, any horror, any difficult time in your life."[1]

When she was a teenager, attending Central High School in Grand Rapids, Michigan, Betty haphazardly whipped a routine together for the annual variety show. After watching the act, Betty's mother told her that she shouldn't perform again unless she was going to do it to the best of her ability.

"These two ideas," Betty says, "form the bookends of how I approach things. If there is something over which you have control and to which you have committed, you must do it to the best of your abilities or not at all. However, when something unexpected happens over which you have no control, you must have the faith to trust that something greater than yourself will guide you."[2]

Wonderful advice from a wonderful lady.

But not easy to follow—especially the part about trust.

Here's a short test for you. Got a pen and a piece of paper? On consecutive lines number from 1 to 12.

Ready?

Next to the numbers write the names of the 12 spies that were sent to scout out Canaan.

1. *Joshua.* (Right!)
2. *Caleb.* (Right again! You're good.)

Why have you stopped writing?

I doubt that you're going to come up with the other names, so let me give them to you:

3. *Shammua*
4. *Shaphat*
5. *Igal*
6. *Palti*
7. *Gaddiel*
8. *Gaddi*
9. *Ammiel*
10. *Sethur*
11. *Nahbi*
12. *Geuel*

In this case two out of twelve isn't bad, actually. (It doesn't show up on the page you're reading, but on my computer screen every one of those 10 names is underscored with a squiggly red line, meaning that even my spell-checker doesn't recognize them.)

Twelve spies. Ten forgotten. Two remembered: the only two who trusted God when they saw the mess they were in.

The other 10 didn't like what they saw. And who could blame them? The cities were fortified. The people were fierce. The soldiers were huge: at eye-level the spies were staring at bellybuttons and belt buckles. Fingering the obsolete weapons dangling from their belts, they did the math. It stacked up to a lopsided fight. Anybody knows you can't kill giants with a slingshot. (Hmmm.)

So they hightailed it home and filed their Report:

> *...the people who live there are fierce, their cities are huge and well fortified. Worse yet, we saw descendants of the giant Anak...We can't attack those people; they're way stronger than we are...Everybody we saw was huge...Alongside them we felt like grasshoppers (Numbers 13:28, 31-33 MSG).*

Here's how I read that report ...

Factual.
Logical.
Realistic.
Sensible.
Faithless!

But don't be too hard on them. They were just doing their job: they were sent to observe, and report back. Based on their observations, and their resources, they were badly overmatched. It was a fight they couldn't win.

But they had forgotten one thing: God had promised to give them this land; promised that he would be with them; promised that nothing could defeat them. There was one sentence that should have been in their report, but wasn't: *Trust in the Lord with all your heart.*

Trust will be Tested

A uniform doesn't tell you if the person wearing it is a fighter or a coward. Even the soldier inside it doesn't know whether he'll stand and fight or turn and run until he faces the enemy and sees which way his feet move.

Trust isn't tested by going to church and listening to sermons. (Longsuffering maybe.) It's tested by battle. It is only in struggle that you find out what you believe and how deeply you believe it.

Here's as good an example as you'll find.

> *"Have you considered my servant Job?"* God asked Satan. *"There is no one on earth like him; he is blameless and upright, a man who fears God and shuns evil"* (Job. 1:8).

Well, why not? Satan snorted. He has it all. Good family. Good friends. Good health. Good job. Good bank balance. You never let anything bad happen to him. Let Mr. Upright get hammered like the poor folks, sick folks, and hurting folks, and he'll curse you.

The hammer dropped. Over and over!

> Thwack … lost his money!
> Thwack … lost his children!
> Thwack … lost his health!

> *"He sends storms to batter and bruise me,"* Job sighed. *"He won't let me catch my breath; he has filled my life with bitterness (Job 9:17-18 TEV).*

But when Job surveyed the wreckage of his ruined life, his trust was bigger than his troubles. His friends attacked his integrity. His wife badgered him to curse God. Job responded, *"Though he slay me, yet will I trust him"* (Job 13:15 NKJV). Trust has seldom stood as tall as it does in that sentence.

Centuries later Peter's hand must have quivered as he jotted this note to his suffering brothers and sisters: *"...it is necessary for you to endure many trials for a while. These trials are only to test your faith..." (1 Peter 1:6-7 NLT)*. A tear splashed on the page as the words he wrote reminded him of the most painful night of his life—the night he failed his Savior.

"Tonight you will all desert me," Jesus told his disciples that night.

"Not me!" said Peter.

"Yes you!" said Jesus. "You'll disown me three times tonight."

"I won't!"

But he did. After Jesus' arrest Peter was pounded with three rapid-fire accusations:

> "You are one of his disciples."
> "I saw you in the garden with him."
> "Your accent gives you away."

Scared senseless, he denied knowing him. Three times.

It's easy to sit in church and sing:

> *I'm so glad I learned to trust Thee,*
> *Precious Jesus, Savior, Friend.*
> *And I know that Thou art with me,*
> *Wilt be with me to the end.*

But trust isn't tested in the pew. It's tested when the night is dark, and cold, and lonely; when loss is devastating, and answers elusive.

Trust will be Honored

Jesus knows the helplessness—and desertion—you feel when your world is falling apart. He knows how it feels to pray and wonder if you're being heard. He's been there. That night in the garden he prayed—once, twice, three times—to be delivered from drinking the cup that had been poured for him.

17

That prayer was answered with cold silence.

Instead of being delivered he was arrested. Instead of being adored he was accused. Instead of being praised he was cursed. Instead of being defended he was thrashed. Instead of being acquitted he was condemned.

Instead of being answered he was ignored.

A few hours later he hung on a cross. Battered. Bloody. Dying.

Had his trust been misplaced? *"He trusts in God,"* scoffers taunted; *"let God deliver him now, if he wants to" (Matthew 27:43 NRSV).*

God still stayed silent.

"My God…why have you forsaken me?" he cried.

But his last breath declared his trust: *"Father, I entrust my spirit into your hands!"*

Three days later God honored that trust with a spine-tingling, heart-stirring, world-changing Sunday.

It was Easter!

Going through tough times?

Trust in the Lord with all your heart.

Easter is coming!

4

WHEN YOU DON'T UNDERSTAND

O n the first night of Hanukkah, 1938, a stooped old man donned his yarmulke and lit the first candle of the menorah, as his father had taught him. His wife and son stood by and watched. "We kindle these lights," he intoned in Hebrew, "on account of the miracles, the deliverances, and the wonders which you did for our fathers."

Father, mother, and son gazed at the lone candle. "That flame," recalled the boy who would become the famous author Chaim Potok, "seemed pitiful against the malignant darkness outside our window."

You see, in 1938 there weren't many miracles, deliverances, or wonders to celebrate. The lingering results of the depression in the United States left little but pain. Far worse, the Jewish world had been shattered as neighborhoods were ravaged, synagogues burned, and Jews herded off to death camps.

The flickering candle seemed impotent to dispel the darkness. Nevertheless, on the next evening the old man lit another candle … and again and again until the eighth night, when one last time he chanted: "We kindle these lights on account of the miracles, the deliverances, and the wonders which you did for our fathers."

Father, mother, and son stood before the glowing menorah. The son stared. The mother sighed. The father spoke: "God doesn't have to live day after day on this broken planet."[1]

The Holocaust was a prime exhibit of "this broken planet."

On November 3, 1943, the Nazis committed simultaneous acts of mass murder in three concentration camps: 43,000 Jewish men, women, and children were executed that day. Those in the Trawniki labor camp were ushered from their barracks in small groups. The first group was commanded to undress and lie down in a pre-dug trench; then they were shot. The next group was forced to undress and lie down on the dead bodies of the first group; then they too were shot. And on it went—group-after-group, layer-on-layer.

Overall, the Holocaust resulted in the slaughter of six million Jews, two-thirds of the nine million Jews living in Europe at the time. How do you measure the scope of this massacre? Imagine the murder of every man, woman, and child in Chicago and you'll be getting close.

Trust Defined

In chapter 1, I told you about the tornado that went on an eight-mile killing rampage in Lubbock, Texas. It skipped Gus Niblack's house, sparing that dear old man and his wife Mary.

I asked the question, "Was Gus singled out by God that night for favorable treatment?" I answered: "I don't know that he was. Or that he wasn't." That answer irks some of my church friends, who are absolutely certain that God did provide special protection for this good man. Perhaps he did.

But let me tell you two more results of that storm that may make you wonder. As it tore across the city, the tornado dipped, demolishing a house where a father and his four-year old son were huddled, killing both. Then it lifted, leaping over the house next door—the one where the drunk lived who had a blood alcohol level of .18 when he killed two teenagers in a head-on collision a month before.

Each day's news offers up a seemingly random delivery of catastrophe, humanly unexplainable.

I stood one afternoon with a grieving man in a windswept West Texas cemetery, where we stared at a casket and an open grave. I was holding my Bible; he was holding two toddlers, one in each arm. His wife, their mother, had lost a brutal battle with cancer. He was left with nothing but memories, bills, and two babies.

These tragedies don't seem to square with the "God Is Love" bumper sticker. If he is all-powerful and could prevent them, why doesn't he? "It's hard to trust a God who would not stop the Holocaust!" hissed the lone survivor of a family of five victims of Hitler's hate.

It's not suffering that troubles us; it's *undeserved* suffering. Those who are thoroughly good suffer as severely as those who are monstrously bad.

That's what threw Job for a loop. He was doing everything right when without warning everything went wrong. His circumstances were as bad as bad can get. And his friends' judgmental sermons were off base. They didn't know the facts behind Job's suffering; nor that God, whom they assumed had abandoned Job, hadn't. (Your conclusions won't be right if your facts are wrong.) These professed friends judged Job and defended God, when Job didn't need to be judged, and God didn't need to be defended.

The book of Job is a blue-ribbon exhibit against religion reduced to simple solutions for painful problems.

> When there is discrepancy between what you believe and what you are experiencing, it's unsettling.

> When you believe that God can heal, that he loves you, and that he answers prayer, yet watch helplessly as your wife dies of cancer, it's confusing.

> When you believe that God is in control of your life, but can't harmonize that belief with a day-after-day assault of unsolvable problems, it's bewildering.

Joseph dreamed that he was destined for greatness—a dream he believed was God-given. He was confident that he would soar to the heights. Instead, he sunk to the depths. Where was God when his brothers sold him into slavery? Where was God when his loyalty to his boss—and to his God—landed him in prison for a crime he didn't commit. His beliefs about God's guidance weren't tracking with his experiences. Still, he trusted.

Later it became clear to Joseph that God had been with him through the whole miserable mess. *"You intended to harm me,"* he said to his brothers, *"but God intended it for good to accomplish what is now being done ..." (Genesis 50:20).*

I have learned more about trust from those who have it than I have from those who write about it. Joseph, Job, and Jesus have defined trust for me—capsuled in three statements:

Joseph: *"You intended to harm me, but God intended it for good ..."*

Job: *"Though he slay me, yet will I trust him."*

Jesus: *"Father, I entrust my spirit into your hands!"*

We wouldn't rush for a front-row seat to hear Joseph deliver a homily on trust back when he was living in luxury, the spoiled son of a wealthy father. But we listen with slack-jawed awe as he declares his trust in the face of betrayal, false accusation, and unjust imprisonment.

We wouldn't walk across the street to hear Job spout aphorisms on trust back when he was the richest man in the world. But he has our undivided attention when he declares his trust-unto-death after he has lost his family, his wealth, and his health.

We wouldn't even be interested in listening to Jesus talk about trust before his earth visit, back when he was on the throne as King of Kings. But we listen in bowed-head reverence when he gasps his trust from the Cross.

From these three I have learned what trust is:

It is certainty that God is in control ...
even when it seems that everything is out of control.

It is certainty that God is doing what is right ...
even when it seems that everything is going wrong.

It is certainty that God is present ...
even when it seems that he is absent.

Joseph, Job, and Jesus defined trust by declaring it, not when things were delightfully good, but when things were terribly bad.

So I hear God asking:

You believe in me when everything is going right.
Would you still trust me if everything was going wrong?

You believe in me when you are prosperous.
Would you still trust me if you lost it all?

You believe in me when you feel my presence.
Would you still trust me if you felt I had forsaken you?

True trust means that you hang on to an unyielding faith in God when things are not going at all like you want them to go: when he doesn't seem supportive; when you feel mistreated, betrayed, abandoned, confused. When you don't understand.

When You Don't Understand

"Trust in the Lord with all your heart," wrote Solomon. But that wasn't his complete sentence. There isn't a period after "heart"—there is a semi-colon (in some translations, a comma), indicating that Solomon wasn't finished. There was more to be said. Here is the rest of his sentence: *"do not depend on your own understanding."*

> *Trust in the Lord with all your heart;*
> *do not depend on your own understanding.*

The examples of suffering I've cited leave us shaking our heads and saying, "I don't understand!"

Exactly!

Your understanding is limited. God's isn't: *"His understanding has no limit" (Psalm 147:5).*

Trust is an acknowledgement of that truth.

He knows what he is doing; you may not. He knows where he is taking you; you may not. And he knows why; you may not.

So through tears, trial, and trouble trust him. Even when you don't understand.

Trust in the Lord with all your heart;
do not depend on your own understanding.

5

WITH YOU ALWAYS

His left arm hung useless at his side, its bones crushed to splinters by the jaws of a lion. Thirty-one times he had been laid low by African fever. It had left its mark; he was thin and pale.

His name was David Livingston. He was speaking at the University of Glasgow, where he was being given an honorary Doctor of Laws degree. Some gasped, others wept, as he described his horrifying experiences on the Dark Continent. You could have heard a pin drop when he declared his intention to return to the land where he had already suffered so much.

"I return," he said, "without misgiving and with great gladness. For I will tell you what supported me through all those years of exile among people whose language I could not understand, and whose attitude towards me was always uncertain and often hostile? It was this: *'Lo, I am with you alway, even unto the end of the world!'* On those words I staked everything, and they never failed!"

On a terrifying evening earlier that year he had been surrounded by savages. Death seemed certain. It was the first time in the sixteen years that he had been in Africa that he had been tempted to abandon his mission and run for safety. But for the thousandth time he turned to the text on which he had staked everything.

Here, read for yourself from his journal.

> January 14, 1856. Felt much turmoil of spirit in prospect
> of having all my plans for the welfare of this great region
> and this teeming population knocked on the head by
> savages …

But I read that Jesus said: "All power is given unto Me in heaven and in earth. Go ye therefore, and teach all nations, and lo, *I am with you alway,* even unto the end of the world."

It is the word of a gentleman of the most strict and sacred honour … I feel quite calm now, thank God!

The words in italics—*I am with you alway*—were underlined in his journal. And in his heart.

Among his last journal entries was this:

He will keep His word … no doubt of it. He will keep His word, and it will be all right.

David Livingston died talking to the companion of his pilgrimage. He was found dead, not on his cot, but on his knees beside it.[1]

I am with you always.

It is a comforting promise, because problems are inevitable. He not only said, *"I am with you always,"* he also said, *"In this world you will have trouble" (John 16:33).*

There is no maybe about it.

Not, "In this world you may occasionally hit a rough patch."
Not, "In this world you may sometimes have pain."
Not, "In this world you *may* have trouble."

No, he is putting you on notice that in this world you *will* have trouble. This world is hostile territory. There is no exemption for saints.

He recruited a dozen men to launch his church. It wasn't a job for wimps. Have a look at the job description.[2]

You will be like sheep in a pack of wolves.
You will be hated.

You will be flogged.

You will be persecuted and put in prison.

You will be betrayed by parents, brothers, relatives, and friends.

You will probably be killed.

And they were—all but one savagely murdered.

They could have avoided the misery. Abandoned the mission. Opted for an easier life. None did. They stuck it out to the end, armed with the promise upon which David Livingston later let his full weight down: *"I am with you always!"*

You have the same promise.

I know, sometimes it doesn't feel like it.

When your companion breaks your marriage vows.

When your child breaks your heart.

When your friend breaks your trust.

No, sometimes it doesn't feel like it. But faith is stronger than feeling. Hang on to your faith that God is working behind the scenes in ways that surpass your understanding.

"Every experience God gives us is preparation for the future that only he can see," said Corrie ten Boom.

Coming from Corrie, that's a sentence worth listening to. When German troops invaded Holland in 1940, the ten Booms built a secret room in their home and began hiding Jews. In 1944 their clandestine activity was discovered. The entire family was arrested and imprisoned.

Casper ten Boom, Corrie's eighty-four year old father, survived only ten days. Corrie was confined to a filthy cell—six steps long and two steps wide—that was already occupied by four women. She and her sister Betsie were soon taken to Ravensbruck, the notorious women's extermination camp in Germany. Betsie died there.

Due to a clerical error, Corrie was released one week before all the women prisoners her age were taken to the gas chambers. She was the only member of her family to survive.

"I wouldn't have chosen the experiences I've had," Corrie said later, "but I wouldn't take anything for them now."

You might choke on the last half of that sentence, but I bet you can say amen to the first half. You could easily draft a list of experiences you've had that you wouldn't have chosen: illnesses, accidents, family crises, financial setbacks, disappointments, shattered dreams—experiences you would have avoided if you could have, but you couldn't. You had to face them and live through them.

You can relate to our earlier discussion of Joseph. The rotten things that happened to him were puzzling and faith-challenging. It was only in hindsight that he saw how God had produced good results out of bad experiences. *"You intended to harm me,"* he said to his brothers, *"but God intended it for good to accomplish what is now being done ..." (Genesis 50:20).*

What is seen as tragedy in your life today may be seen as triumph when ripened by time. The distressing circumstances you are facing in this life may be reclassified as gifts of grace in the next one. With heavenly hindsight you may see blessings in experiences that you wouldn't have chosen.

It's an old story, and I don't know the source of it, but here is the way I remember it ...

A Chinese farmer had one son and one horse. One day the horse broke out of the corral and ran into the hills. The farmer's neighbor said, "Your horse ran away. What bad luck!" The farmer replied, "Maybe, maybe not."

The next day the horse returned, leading twelve wild stallions. The neighbor said, "Now you have thirteen horses. What good luck!" The farmer replied, "Maybe, maybe not."

A few days later, while trying to break one of the stallions, the farmer's son was thrown off and broke his leg. The neighbor said, "Your son broke his leg. What bad luck!" The farmer replied, "Maybe, maybe not."

The next day a Chinese warlord came through town and drafted all able-bodied young men, taking them off to a war from which most never returned. Because he had a broken leg, the farmer's son wasn't drafted.

Whether what happens today is good or bad can only be measured by time.

That Friday when Jesus died seemed like a very bad day; history's worst by far. But in fact it was the day when God's greatest gift of grace was given. By the fourth century that bad Friday was being celebrated as Good Friday. And has been ever since.

Life's events can only be judged by stepping back from the moment and hearing, as Emerson said, "what the centuries say against the years."

We see years. God sees centuries—and more.

Your time here is just the first few days of a very long life, as in *everlasting*. Don't grade the never-ending by these first few days.

When it seems that you're all alone, you aren't! *"I am with you always!"*

> *Trust in the Lord with all your heart;*
> *do not depend on your own understanding.*

Summary Resolutions from Section One

TRUST

Trust in the Lord with all your heart;
do not depend on your own understanding.
—Proverbs 3:5

I RESOLVE to be grateful for the Giver, not just for the gifts.

I RESOLVE to remain faithful when He doesn't answer my prayers the way I want Him to—or as quickly as I want Him to.

I RESOLVE to remember that everything that happens in my life is preparation for a future that only He can see.

I RESOLVE to trust Him unconditionally, however difficult the problem, however elusive the answer.

I RESOLVE to remember that when it seems I am all alone, I'm not.

I RESOLVE to stand firm on His promise: "I am with you always."

SECTION TWO

ASSURANCE

… (He) is able to do immeasurably more
than all we ask or imagine …
—EPHESIANS 3:20

When you pass through the waters, I will be with you; and when you pass through the rivers, they will not sweep over you … Do not be afraid, for I am with you (Isaiah 43:2, 5).

❧

Hurricane season runs from June 1 to November 30 in my neck of the woods. Every night during those six months a segment of the 10 o'clock news focuses on ocean threats, often hundreds of miles from our coast.

Print media tries to outdo TV with its daily warnings, keeping nerves raw. At the beginning of this year's season a big-name weather journalist served up this paragraph:

> Here we stand on the doorstep of the Atlantic hurricane season, by most predictions a season promising twice as many tropical storms as normal, with one forecast calling for five major hurricanes to form. We all know it only takes one.

My bet is that medical supply stores did big business in blood pressure cuffs the day that column ran.

But our worries about weather are minor compared to the life storms we dream up …

> With my luck they'll raise taxes to 65% and the beginning age for Social Security to 85.

> My daughter will probably show up dragging a dude with spiked green hair and a lip ring and say, "Guess what?"

> I've had a sore throat for a week—cancer of the larynx no doubt.

Fear of gathering storms—real or imagined—whips up hand-wringing anxiety.

When storms threaten, you need assurance: assurance of his presence and assurance of his power.

You have both.

Do not be afraid, for I am with you.
(He) is able to do immeasurably more than all we ask or imagine …

6

GOD, GARLIC, AND GADGETS

As I pulled to a stop at the traffic light I spotted them loitering at the corner of the campus—a knot of clean-cut kids, wearing identical T-shirts. Stenciled on front: *Klein Bearkats Basketball.* On back: *Refuse to Lose.*

The Bearkats usually win.

Those who expect to win generally do. And those who lose can often chalk it up to the fact that they expected to. We tend to live up to our expectations. When high expectations fire the furnace of the human spirit, it's astonishing what people achieve.

But expectations do more than fill win-and-loss columns. They regulate attitudes, and emotions, and relationships. And they are self-fulfilling prophecies. More often than not you see what you expect to see; hear what you expect to hear; feel what you expect to feel.

If you expect to be mistreated, you probably will be—or think you are.

If you expect to dislike a person, you likely will.

If you expect people to be hostile, that's what you'll feel.

If you expect them to be friendly, that's what you'll sense.

If you expect the church to be cold and uncaring, that's what you will perceive it to be.

If you expect it to be uplifting and nurturing, that's what you will experience.

35

If you expect something to go badly, chances are it will.

If you expect it to go well, most likely that's what will happen.

Here's another thing about expectations: when you expect God's involvement, you eliminate the negative. You expect a positive outcome, because even when present circumstances are lousy, you know that God is good at writing happy endings.

An old maxim runs this way: "When you come to the end of your rope, tie a knot and hang on!" Paul got himself into a terrible mess in Ephesus. Here's his report:

> *We were really crushed and overwhelmed, and feared we would never live through it. We felt we were doomed to die and saw how powerless we were to help ourselves; but that was good, for then we put everything into the hands of God ... And he did help us ... and we expect him to do it again and again (2 Corinthians 1:8-11 TLB).*

Now that's what I call tying a knot and hanging on! When doom seemed certain, Paul put everything into the hands of God, and hung on for dear life. God came through. "And we expect him to do it again and again," Paul said. How's that for high expectations?

Maybe he had read these words:

> *In the morning, O Lord, you hear my voice; in the morning I lay my requests before you and wait in expectation (Psalm 5:3).*

Don't grab your remote and start your day with negative news. Talk to your Father and start your day with positive prospects.

Paul wrapped it in one powerful sentence: *He is able to do immeasurably more than all we ask or imagine.*

When I was a child, my father was able to reach things that I couldn't, because he was taller than I was. He was able to lift things that I couldn't, because he was stronger than I was. He was able do things that I couldn't, because he was smarter than I was.

I thought my father could do anything. He couldn't. But my Father can.

My father had limitations. But my Father doesn't.

God, Garlic, and Gadgets

Over a half-century ago J.B. Phillips wrote a little book titled *Your God is too Small,* in which he sketched common conceptions of God ... one of those being a God who is distant and disinterested, unable and unreachable. We don't expect much from a God like that.

But we expect a lot from a God like Paul pictures: one who is able to do more than all we can ask or imagine. A God without limitations. A God who specializes in the impossible.

The surface outside the back gate of my apartment complex is nothing but dirt, unless it has rained recently—like it did last night. Then it's mud! I blew a serious slice of time this morning cleaning my shoes ... and grumbling. But my grumbling didn't change the law: when dirt and water mix, they make mud. There is no exception to that law.

Well, actually there is.

The Israelites were running for their lives, with Pharaoh's troops in hot pursuit. Looking over their shoulders these runaway slaves were terrified. When they didn't think things could get any worse, they did: their escape was blocked by the Red Sea. Pharaoh couldn't have hoped for more. He had them right where he wanted them. Hopelessly trapped! Sea in front, soldiers in back.

"Do not be afraid," Moses shouted. *"Stand firm and you will see the deliverance the Lord will bring you today" (Exodus 14:13).* Clearly he'd lost his mind. A body of water twelve miles wide and a half-mile deep isn't exactly a wading pool. If he had said, "Let's get on our knees and ask God

to get us to the other side of this sea," he wouldn't have had enough takers to fill a pew for a Wednesday night prayer-meeting. They couldn't see any way out of this mess.

Then the wind started blowing and the sea started parting—and two million Jews trotted across the sea bed on dry ground (Exodus 14:22). Not mud, mind you. Dry ground!

How's that for pulling off the impossible?! Pretty good, I'd say.

They thought so, too: *"When the Israelites saw the great power the Lord displayed against the Egyptians, the people … put their trust in him and in Moses his servant" (Exodus 14:31)*. They even composed a celebratory song. The first verse went this way: *"I will sing to the Lord, for he has triumphed gloriously."* And the last verse ran: *"The Lord will reign for ever and ever" (Exodus 15:1, 18)*.

Know how long that *for ever and ever* lasted? Three days! That's how long it took for them to start fussing that the water was bitter and the food was disgusting. *"We remember the fish we ate in Egypt at no cost,"* they howled—*"also the cucumbers, melons, leeks, onions and garlic."*[1] (Having been repeatedly nailed to the foyer wall by a blast of sister Gandry's eye-crossing garlic breath, I'm at a loss to understand why garlic was on the Israelite's list of dietary cravings. But to each her own.)

It was impossible to please this mob. The Red Sea triumph was impressive … but their awe faded fast.

We may be even harder to impress. After all, we've seen some remarkable developments in our lifetime. I carry an electronic gadget in my pocket that's smaller than your wallet. It's a telephone, a text-messenger, an address book, an appointment calendar, a memo pad, a voice recorder, a camera, and an alarm clock—all wrapped up in this one little gizmo. It also sends and receives my email, and lets me access the internet.

Am I impressed? Kinda, but not very. Amazing things have happened so fast and so often in my lifetime that I'm hard to impress. Any new gadget that I need is soon to be released.

But there comes a time when garlic and gadgets don't cut it. They can't do much for you when you have cancer, suffer a heart-breaking loss, or lose a loved one. That's when you need more than garlic and gadgets; you need God.

Man does the amazing. God does the impossible.

> *... my thoughts are not your thoughts, neither are your ways my ways ... As the heavens are higher than the earth, so are my ways higher than your ways and my thoughts than your thoughts (Isaiah 55:8-9).*

The Answer to Your Question

When you face a perplexing, seemingly hopeless, situation, you may have a question or two.

Moses did. When the cranky horde he was leading squawked that they wanted meat, Moses growled, "Where am I supposed to get it?" God said, "I'll provide it." *"I'm standing here surrounded by 600,000 men"* Moses retorted, *"and you say, 'I'll give them meat ....'"* Moses' question was, *"So where's it coming from?" (Numbers 11:21 MSG).* Good question.

Mary had a question. When the angel told her that she was going to have a baby, her question was, *"How can this be, since I am a virgin?" (Luke 1:34).* Good question.

Andrew had a question. Jesus blindsided his disciples late one afternoon by ordering them to feed 5,000 hungry men on a far-from-the-market mountainside. A crowd-canvass came up with a total of one sack lunch, consisting of five biscuits and two fish. Andrew's question was, *"How far will they go among so many?" (John 6:9).* Good question.

What's your question?

> How do I get out of this financial mess I'm in?
> How do I endure this miserable marriage?
> How do I deal with this out-of-control child?

How do I handle my hatred of that person?
How do I defeat this debilitating addiction?
How do I conquer this temptation that I repeatedly yield to?

Jesus gave a one-sentence answer: *"What is impossible with men is possible with God"* (Luke 18:27).

That was the answer for Moses, and Mary, and Andrew. And it's the answer for you.

There are three doxologies in the New Testament that start by saying *he is able ...*

> Jude has one that begins: *"To him who is able to keep you from falling and to present you before his glorious presence without fault ..."* (Jude 24).

> Paul has one that begins: *"Now to him who is able to strengthen you ...* (Romans 16:25 RSV).

> And then Paul has this one that begins: *"Now to him who is able to do immeasurably more than all we ask or imagine"* (Ephesians 3:20).

He is able. He is able. He is able.

If these verses aren't working in your life, it isn't because you haven't read the right book or attended the right seminar, it's because you haven't tapped into the right power.

These affirmations imply not only his ability, but also his willingness. He wouldn't tell you that he is able unless there was an underlying promise that he is willing.

Your Biography isn't Finished

Unanswered prayer seems to have only one father: God. (I've never heard anyone fret, "Why doesn't luck answer my prayer?")

Answered prayer, on the other hand, has many fathers: talent; timing; luck; coincidence.

Maybe you've heard about the chap who was in a sweat because he was running late for an important meeting. He had cruised the block for a quarter-hour, searching in vain for a parking spot. Finally he prayed, "God, I really need to make this meeting, and I'm running out of time. If you will find me a parking space I promise to go to church every Sunday, and to quit cussing." Voilà! There it was! An open spot, ten steps from the front door of his meeting location. "Never mind, God," he said, "I found one."

But you're not like that. You believe, really believe, that God hears and answers prayer, right? You are beyond doubting. You believe, really believe, that God is able to do what you ask, because you have experienced it. You have measured the problems that you have faced by the prayers that you have prayed, and know without a doubt that God intervened. And so you set prayer over against the challenges that you are presently facing, or may face: illness, divorce, financial setback, devastating loss, whatever. And you believe, really believe, that God will stand alongside you and see you through. And when things are not working out as you want them to, you keep praying, because you believe, really believe, that God is able.

And he is.

Tough times? Don't give up! Don't put a period where God puts a comma ... your biography isn't finished yet.

He is able to do more than all you ask or imagine.

41

7

THE ALL-SEEING EYE

Lydia King's grandson was broke and homesick. His new job in California was a long way from his Pennsylvania home. So Lydia was planning to head west to do what grandmas do—slip him a few bucks and stock his fridge with comfort food. And did she ever have a surprise for him—a brand-new red Toyota Corolla! She would drive the car to California, do the grandma thing, then fly back to Philadelphia.

Three days before she was scheduled to hit the road Lydia slipped and hit the floor. Broke her arm. The doctor tried to convince her to postpone the trip. Nothin' doin'! A broken bone and an uptight doc was no match for this feisty grandma. So he plastered the arm in a wrist-to-elbow cast, gave her a prescription for pain pills, wrote his office and home phone numbers on the cast, and wished her luck.

Three days into the trip Lydia was sagging, so she stopped for a shot of caffeine at a roadside diner in Oklahoma. As she headed back to her car, a stranger approached. "Are you driving a red Toyota with Pennsylvania dealer plates?" he asked.

Lydia froze. Seeing her fear, he backed off a couple of steps, assured her that he meant no harm, and explained the reason for his question. Three days ago, he said, a truck driver in Pennsylvania had noticed a little white-haired lady with a cast on her arm, driving alone. Truckers, communicating with CBs and cell phones, had been keeping track of her ever since, ready to help if she had a problem. When she stopped at night the location was reported. When she got on the road the next morning, the nearest trucker commenced the day's guardianship, passing her off to another driver when he had to stop.

When Lydia took the exit ramp for her coffee break she was in the tailing trucker's blind spot. After driving several miles without seeing her, he broadcast his concern. No problem—another driver had just spotted her car in the diner parking lot.

Lydia had driven over 1,200 miles, unaware that this guardian-brigade was watching over her. She was stunned. And grateful.

That All-Seeing Eye

Watching yoooouuu, waatching yoouuu,
There's an all-seeing eye watching yoouu.

I hated that song.

I grew up thinking that God had his eye on me, just waiting to catch me in some sin. He saw everything I did, heard everything I said, even knew everything I was thinking. Yikes! He was frowning, shaking his head, and making notes in his black book. It reminded me of another song …

There's a great day coming, a great day coming;
There's a great day coming by and by,
When the saints and the sinners shall be parted right and left,
Are you ready for that day to come?

Gulp! The great day was coming when he would call my name, open his book to my page, and I would have to face the music. It scared the daylights out of me.

The Ten Commandments and Eight Beatitudes are all we need to read to know that we're sunk! The all-seeing eye has nailed us.

I haven't sung *Watching You* in a long time. But I could sing it today with a smile on my face and joy in my heart, because my take on those words is different now than it was at those long-ago Sunday afternoon singings. God is watching over me just like those truckers were watching over Lydia King—to protect me, not to catch me breaking the speed limit.

You carefully observe me when I travel or when I lie down to rest; you are aware of everything I do (Psalm 139:3 NET).

There isn't a mile or a moment when God isn't watching out for you.
Not a mile or a moment when he isn't concerned about you.
Not a mile or a moment when you are alone.
The setting for the movie *The Legend of Bagger Vance* is a thirty-six-hole exhibition match between two golfing legends, Bobby Jones and Walter Hagen, at Krewe Island, Georgia. Rannulph Junah, a tormented local war hero, once a golf-great himself, is added to the card as an honorary participant.

Junah surprises the guest big guns and the gallery by starting stronger than expected. But on the second day, haunted by combat memories, he starts falling apart and falling behind.

Bagger Vance, Junah's mystic mentor and caddie, pulls him aside and says, "Ain't a soul in this entire earth ain't got a burden to carry that he can't understand. You ain't alone in that, but you have been carrying this one long enough. It's time to lay it down."

"I can't!" Junuh protests.

"Oh, yes you can," Bagger replies. "You are not alone. I am right here with you. I have been all along. Now, play the game, your game—the one that you were meant to play."

Past memories and present problems may be haunting and paralyzing you. You can't think straight. You can hardly breathe. You feel like you are all alone. But you're not.

When you pass through the waters, I will be with you; and when you pass through the rivers, they will not sweep over you. … Do not be afraid, for I am with you (Isaiah 43:2, 5).

"Ain't a soul in this entire earth ain't got a burden to carry that he can't understand. You ain't alone in that, but you have been carrying this one long enough. It's time to lay it down."

Time for you to rely on his power and count on his presence. Time to reach for heavenly help. *"When you are in trouble, call out to me. I will answer and be there ... "* *(Psalm 91:15 CEV).*

When You Ask, and Even When You Don't

I recently enjoyed guided tours of two places that I had wanted to see for a long time: the Johnson Space Center and the Houston Astros' Minute Maid Park. It piqued my curiosity—what would a guided tour of heaven be like?

Our angel-guide would no doubt call attention to many things we have read about—gates of pearl, golden streets, many mansions. And to a few things we have never even thought about ...

"What's in there?" you ask, pointing to a stadium-size warehouse.

"Gifts never given. Blessings never received," responds our angel-guide—"answers to prayers never prayed."

Here are some folks who didn't leave their blessings in a bin in that warehouse.

"Lord," a high-ranking army officer said to Jesus, "my servant lies at home paralyzed and in terrible suffering."

"I'll come and heal him," Jesus said.

"I am not worthy to have you come into my home," said the soldier. "Just say the word from where you are, and my servant will be healed."

"It will be done just as you believed it would," Jesus said. And the servant was healed that very moment (Matthew 8:5-13).

Then two blind men came to him, begging for mercy. "Do you believe that I am able to do this?" Jesus asked them. "Yes, Lord," they replied. "According to your faith will it be done" he said (Matthew 9:29). And suddenly they saw.

They believed. They asked. They received.

But our fictitious heavenly dialogue didn't get it altogether right. God doesn't just give when we ask—he often gives when we don't; does more than we ask or imagine when we neither ask nor imagine.

The bookends of Israel's forty-year desert trek were blessings they didn't ask for.

When they left Egypt and entered the desert God gave them a dry ground crossing of the Red Sea. They didn't ask for it, because it never occurred to them that he could give it. He could, and he did.

Forty years later, when they left the desert and entered the Promised Land he gave them a dry ground crossing of the Jordan. They didn't ask for it, because it never occurred to them that he could give it. He could, and he did.

Dry ground crossings when they entered the desert and when they left it. Neither asked for.

Has he given you blessings that you haven't asked for? You wouldn't have lived to read this sentence if he hadn't.

Did you ask for oxygen any time in the past twenty-four hours? Didn't think so.

Did you put in a request for blood-flow today? Your brain amounts to a tiny fraction of your total body weight—only three pounds. But it consumes 20% of your blood supply. If blood-flow to your brain was cut off for 10 seconds, you would lose consciousness. If it was cut off three to five minutes you would have permanent brain damage.[1]

Did you spend prayer time this morning asking for what keeps you anchored to terra firma? Gravity! You would be floating in space, sans spacesuit, without it.

It wouldn't take much thought to make a lengthy list of good things that you have received that you didn't ask for.

Ready when You Are

If your prayer life is anything like mine, you hit dry patches now and then. You *try* to pray. You think you *should* pray. But you don't feel like

47

praying. You've already said everything you know to say—more than once. Or you don't know how to say what you want to say. Or you're just not in the mood to pray.

Not to worry. God is still there, and he isn't going anywhere. When you're ready to talk again, he is ready to listen. He is watching out for you. Always happy to hear from you …

and able to do more than you ask or imagine.

8

THE HARDEST PRAYER TO PRAY

Here is a question I've asked a dozen preachers over the past few months: "How much of God do the people who fill your pews on Sunday want in their lives?"

Each has been quick to say that some of his sheep are completely committed. God is everything to them. He comes first. There isn't a close second.

But these are far outnumbered, they've said, by those who want God in their lives, but not too much of him.

> Not so much that it interferes with their schedule.
> Not so much that it conflicts with their business.
> Not so much that it horns in on their leisure.
> Not so much that it clashes with their lifestyle.
> Not so much that it tempts them to tithe—perish the thought!

It's not that church membership isn't important to them. It is. When their names show up in the obituaries they want it to be clear that they were members in good standing. One minister confided that of the 17 memorial services he had conducted in the past year, 14 of the death notices cited the deceased's devotion to the church. But he opined that if God read the obits, he would respond to half of those postings by asking, "Who?"

These ministers feel that a lot of their members want a relationship with God, but don't want him to get too close. A little bit of God is good, but don't get carried away and slap a "God Loves You" bumper-sticker on your car.

A once-a-week God seems to be about the right amount for some of us … until we're up to our armpits in trouble. Then we want more. Want to get closer. Want to pray, but hardly know how to.

Pray any way you choose. God is always happy to hear from you. But prayer that works best is prayer that puts God first. "The Lord's Prayer" is the model. The first half of that prayer exalts God; the last half requests help.

Our Father in heaven,	**God First**
hallowed be your name,	
your kingdom come,	His name
your will be done	His kingdom
on earth as it is in heaven.	His will
Give us today our daily bread.	**Requests Second**
Forgive us our debts, as we also	
have forgiven our debtors.	Give us
And lead us not into temptation,	Forgive us
but deliver us from the evil one.	Deliver us
—Matthew 6:9-13	

What is the hardest part of that prayer to pray? See if my take on it tracks with yours.

The hardest part is not *"hallowed be your name."* I grew up in a home where God's name was revered, so I came by this part without much effort.

The hardest part is not *"Give us today our daily bread."* Millions go hungry. I have never been one of them, so I—without much thought and with too little gratitude—take daily bread for granted.

The hardest part is not *"forgive us … as we also have forgiven …"* Don't get me wrong—I could name a person or two that I think should have to undergo a root canal without pain-killer as a pre-condition of forgiveness. Still, that's not the hardest part of the prayer for me to pray.

Know what is?

"Your will be done!"

That's the hardest part. Not the hardest part to say, but the hardest part to mean.

You see, I, for the most part, pray that *my* will be done. Don't you? Don't you usually pray for what you want to occur—and ask God to make it happen?

If you can pray, and really mean, *"your will be done,"* you will be okay with whatever answer he gives, because you will be certain that he will do what is best.

Conflicting Requests

God gets conflicting requests.

Most of my church ministry was spent in West Texas, where cotton is king. Cotton needs water. Every drop of the average annual West Texas rainfall of 18½ inches was crucial. So it got a little dicey when July rolled around and the rain gauge had measured a measly three inches for the year. After a Sunday service it was common for one of our weather-toughened farmers to say, "Pray for rain, preacher!"

That put me in a pinch for two reasons.

First, the Bible says *"The prayer of the righteous is powerful and effective."* If I prayed for rain and it didn't rain I would come off looking bad, don't you think—somewhere south of righteous? (Quit frowning. I'm kidding.)

Second (I'm not kidding now), I had a friend who was in commercial construction. If he finished a project behind schedule he faced a per diem penalty. It didn't take many lost workdays to axe his profit and land him on the wrong side of the ledger. (You're ahead of me, aren't you?) While my farmer friends needed rain, that was the last thing my construction friend needed. A spoken prayer to bless the farmer was an unspoken prayer to break the builder.

The setting for Mark Twain's *The War Prayer* was a church filled with soldiers, and their families and friends. The troops were set to leave for the front the following day. Visions of the battle were vivid in the minds of all: flashing sabers, fierce combat, and hopefully victory and the safe return of their fighting men.

The minister's prayer was long and passionate. Bless our soldiers. Crush our foe. Uphold our land and flag!

During the prayer a stranger entered the building and quietly made his way to the front. When the preacher's prayer ended, the stranger spoke. He said that two prayers had been prayed, not one—one spoken, the other unspoken.

He put the unspoken prayer into words. Help us tear their soldiers to bloody shreds. Cover their fields with their patriot dead. Drown the sounds of the guns with the shrieks of their wounded. Destroy their humble homes. Fill the hearts of their widows with grief. Cause their children to suffer hunger and thirst and wander in rags.

It was a sobering reminder that a prayer for their victory was a prayer for someone else's defeat; a prayer for their joy, a prayer for someone else's sorrow.

God has children on both sides of the trenches. Sometimes with conflicting requests.

Trombones and Saxophones

I played trombone in my high school band. The only sheet of music that mattered to me was the one on my stand.

The day after the biggest concert of my senior year there was a glowing write-up in the school paper:

> The band's final number, John Philip Sousa's *Stars and Stripes Forever,* brought the audience to its feet. The trombone section was especially brilliant.

Clearly the girl who wrote that column was destined for journalistic greatness—I could see a Pulitzer in her future.

Sadly, the trombones weren't always featured. I hated it when my music showed measure-after-measure of rests: *put your horn on your knee and sit this one out, Bubba.* When the spotlight shifted from me to the saxophone player I was a little irritated. Bitter? You might say that. I didn't like his smug saxo*phony* smile.

The first time I saw the band director's score I was stunned. The sheet on my stand had only my part. His had line after line of staffs, showing the parts for every instrument in the band. His job was to bring all of those parts together; blend them into a harmonious whole.

God is the maestro who has to pull all the pieces of our world together. It's not all about you. You can't always be the soloist. Sometimes the saxophones need his attention.

It's not easy to let him call the shots, to pray *"Your will be done"* when what prompted you to pray was the desire that your will be done. But when your prayer life reaches that level of maturity you have the promise of answered prayer: *"If we ask anything according to his will he hears us"* (1 *John 5:14).*

He hears!

And *he is able to do more than all you ask or imagine.*

53

9

LISTEN FOR HIS VOICE

"You can be anything you want to be!"

"You can do anything you want to do!"

Not true!

I know, your mother told you over and over that you could be anything you wanted to be and do anything you wanted to do. So did your favorite teacher. And your Aunt Sophie.

But, with all due respect, it's just not so!

At 5-10 and 150 pounds, playing linebacker for the Green Bay Packers wasn't in my future.

I had a friend who pictured himself as the next Frank Sinatra. If desire and hard work could put one in the game he would have said "Hellooooo Vegas!" But, blunt truth is that his voice would send people running for the Exits in a Karaoke Bar.

Don't get me wrong. Many people work past problems, overcome handicaps, ignore naysayers, push themselves to the limit, and by refuse-to-quit effort reach goals that seem unreachable. I admire that.

But be *anything* you want to be? Do *anything* you want to do? Huh-uh!

But here's something to get excited about: you can be anything God wants you to be, and do anything God wants you to do, because he will give you the abilities that match the tasks that he wants you to take on. He has often chosen people for jobs they didn't apply for—and couldn't see themselves filling.

> He chose an insignificant shepherd boy to be Israel's greatest king.

He chose a dozen seemingly ordinary men to launch his church.

He chose a church butcher to be a church builder; the chief of sinners became the chief of saints.

He even chose a murderer and coward to deliver his people from slavery.

This one-sentence eulogy of that remarkable man says it all: *"No one has ever shown the mighty power or performed the awesome deeds that Moses did" (Deuteronomy 34:12).*

But that's the way he finished, not the way he started. His start was unremarkable. He was minding his own business when God drafted him to take care of *his* business. "I've seen the misery of my people in Egypt," God said, "and I am concerned about their suffering. I am sending you to get them out of there."

C'mon! Moses was a shepherd, not a soldier. Besides, he was a fugitive from Egypt, wanted for murder. Swagger across the border where there's a warrant for your arrest? Get real! Moses knew all about Egypt and Pharaoh: scary place, scary king.

So Moses came back at God with a little Q&A.[1]

Q: Why me? I'm not the right person for this job.
A: I will be with you!

Q: If I go to the Israelites and say, "God has sent me," and they ask me, "What is his name?" What do I tell them?
A: Tell them, "I AM has sent me. The God of your fathers—the God of Abraham, the God of Isaac and the God of Jacob—has sent me to you."

Q: I'm not good with words. Never have been. I stutter. You need to find someone else.

A: That's a statement, not a question. Here's a plan—I'll send your brother with you. He's a smoothie. We'll let him do the talking. Now, you have a long trip and a big job ahead of you, so get packed and get going.

You know the rest of the story. Moses got Israel out of Egypt, and led them for 40 years. Rough patches? You bet, lots of them. But in his retirement speech, he passed the baton of leadership to Joshua with a couple of sentences that summarized that 40-year experience: *"The Lord himself goes before you and will be with you; he will never leave you nor forsake you. Do not be afraid; do not be discouraged"* (Deuteronomy 31:8).

God chose Moses.

And God chose you. There is something he wants you to be, and something he wants you to do. He will give you everything you need to be that and do that. The clay doesn't argue with the potter about how he is shaping it. It yields to the potter to shape as it pleases him.[2] God has made you exactly what he wants you to be.

Things that Can't be Changed—and Things that Can

In the summer of 1934, Dr. Reinhold Niebuhr was vacationing in Heath, Massachusetts. While there he accepted an invitation to preach at a nearby church one Sunday. He concluded his sermon with this prayer:

God, give us Grace to accept with Serenity the things that cannot be changed.

Courage to change the things that should be changed,

And Wisdom to distinguish the one from the other.

A visitor asked Dr. Niebuhr if he might make a copy of that prayer. Niebuhr pulled the scrap of paper on which he had jotted the prayer from his Bible and handed it to him. "You may have this," he said.

The man enclosed the prayer with his Christmas letter that year, and from that small mailing it began a worldwide journey, becoming one of the most-quoted prayers in history.

It's easy to see why. In two sentences Niebuhr homed in on two issues that we all grapple with: things that can't be changed, and things that can be.

Some things can't be changed, no matter how much you wish they could: an unwanted divorce, an illness that won't yield to treatment, the death of a loved one—situations that Paul Tillich described as "what we come up against and have to adjust to because we realize they will not adjust to us."

On the other hand, some things can be changed. You, for instance. Don't forget, there is something God wants you to be, and something that he wants you to do. But it may take you awhile to get there. You have to grow into it. You are not a finished product, but a work in progress; still being shaped, still in the process of becoming.

There may be some things in your life that should be—and, with God's help, can be—changed. A bad habit, perhaps. Maybe a cynical attitude, or a touchy disposition. Have a hard look at yourself. Are you on the right track? Are you using your rapidly-passing life well? It's never too late to ask these questions. And never too late to change the answers.

Take the initiative, but realize that you're not in this alone. Assurance of his presence and power will give you serenity in the painful stretches of life that can't be changed, and the courage to tackle the things that can be.

Listen for His Voice

They were feeling such loss. They had expected so much and walked away with so little. They had thought that by now they would be cabinet members in a new administration, thwarting Rome's rule and restoring Israel's independence. Instead, they were jobless, and Rome was having her way.

With heavy hearts and sluggish steps they had come home, to Galilee. "I'm going fishing," Peter said. Six pals chimed in, "We're going with you." These guys didn't fish for fun. Fishing was their occupation—or had been before they hooked up with Jesus. It's what they were doing the day he showed up and said, "Follow me." And they did. They berthed their boat, mothballed their nets, and became his disciples. He taught them. Inspired them. Seeded their dream for a never-ending kingdom. Never-ending? The campaign collapsed before the kingdom commenced! He was arrested. Convicted. Now he was dead!

So it was back to their old job. They unpacked their nets, boarded their boat, and started rowing. Out in familiar water they tossed the net. Bad throw. They hadn't fished for three years, and were out of practice. When they finally got the hang of it they threw it over and over, all night long, without netting a single fish. Not only had their hopes for position and power been dashed, they'd even lost their job skills.

Peter looked at John. "Did you say something?" he asked.

"No."

"You, James?"

"No, I didn't say anything."

"Nathanael?"

"Wasn't me."

Cupping a hand behind his ear, John said, "Shh. Listen! Hear that voice? It's coming from the beach."

"Any fish, boys? Throw your net on the right side of the boat and you'll get plenty of them."

John's stomach turned flips! He could barely breathe. He was having a flashback. It was as vivid as if it had been yesterday, though it had occurred three years ago. They had fished all night, and come back with an empty boat. They were putting away their nets when Jesus stepped into their boat and said, *"Put out into deep water, and let down the nets for a catch."* They did—and caught so many fish their nets started ripping.[3]

The voice coming from the shore had to be his!

"It is the Lord!" John said.

And sure enough, it was![4]

Does any of this feel familiar? Have I caught you at a time when you're feeling down? Disappointed because things haven't worked out the way you hoped they would? Tempted to go back to your old life—fishing for whatever it was you fished for before you met him?

Listen for his voice. Is he telling you to throw your net on the other side of the boat? Telling you to do something different than what you've been doing? Think of one thing that you think he wants you to do differently. One thing that you think he wants you to change.

Listen for his voice. And do what he says. The catch will be bigger than you can imagine.

He is able to do more than all you ask or imagine.

10

GOD'S "MORE"

I have never met Sue, but the letter I received from her made me wish I had. She had reason to be bitter, but wasn't.

She and Clarence wanted children—four of them. But their first six years of marriage yielded four miscarriages instead of four children. Each time Sue got far enough into the pregnancy that it showed. Each time friends gushed their congratulations. And each time she lost her baby.

After the fourth miscarriage, the doctor said that Sue's health was at risk. They should give up trying to have children.

"One more time," she said to Clarence as they left the hospital … "Let's try one more time."

So they did. It was a picture-perfect, problem-free pregnancy. Sue was on cloud nine. She was going to have this baby! She just knew it.

And she did. Baby Robby was born. With Down syndrome.

The doctor was brutally blunt: Robby would never be able to feed himself, tie his shoes, or go to school. Sue sat by Robby's crib and sobbed for hours.

Clarence went for take-out, and never came back.

Heartbreak times two: handicapped baby; cop-out husband.

Sue had no money, no job skills, and no idea how she was going to raise this special-needs child all by herself.

Rough days came, lots of them. But so did good ones. Sue cleaned houses and took classes, and eventually got a degree and a decent job. Robby had cognitive and physical limitations, but contrary to the doctor's insensitive prognostication, he fed himself, tied his shoes, and went to school. And he had a beautifully sweet disposition. He was indeed a "special" child.

"It might have been nice," Sue wrote, "having normal children and a husband by my side as they grew up and I grew old. That's the way it has been for most of my friends. Some of them are happy, some aren't.

"I didn't get the life I'd hoped for, but I can tell you without reservation that if I could trade the life I have for the one I thought I wanted, I'd pass. I wouldn't trade a single day I've had with Robby for a lifetime of my youthful dreams. God knew what Robby needed—me. And he knew what I needed—Robby. He has given me more than I could have ever imagined."

Like Sue, you may have hit some potholes; traveled seemingly endless stretches of rough road that you'd have given anything to have avoided. You may be navigating that road at this very moment. Even though it seems the agony will last forever, it won't. One of these days the road will turn and the scenery will change. As Sue said, God is able to do more than you can imagine.

That's what Paul said, too: *He is able to do immeasurably more than all we ask or imagine (Ephesians 3:20).*

It is only fair to warn you that the word in that sentence that may give you the most trouble is "more." It's the word you think you like most, but may turn out to be the one you like least.

C'mon, Joe. I would be thrilled to get more than I asked for!

Sounds good, doesn't it? He is able to take what you ask for, and enlarge it. His "more" may be a generous add-on to your request.

You've experienced that, haven't you? You asked. And his answer included far more than you asked for. You hit pay dirt. Won the lottery. Nailed the prize.

That's great!

But it may not be the whole story.

God's "More"

God's "more" may be—and here's what you may not like—it may be something different than what you asked for. Your heart is set on what you asked for. If he gives you something different, you may be unable to see it as anything other than rejection.

When Paul wrote that God is able to do more than we ask or imagine, he was writing out of personal experience. God's answers to his prayers included more than he had asked for—a "more" that probably puzzled and disappointed him. It didn't seem that his prayer had been answered at all. Let me show you ...

Paul planned to preach in Asia, but the Holy Spirit vetoed it (Acts 16:6). So he altered his plan—he would turn north, to Asia Minor. But that got a thumbs down too (Acts 16:7). He had run out of land—there was nowhere else to go. Unless ...

Standing at the edge of the Aegean Sea, two hundred miles of water separating him from the opposite shore, the call was clear: go to Europe. That wasn't remotely what he had planned on or prayed for. Worked out pretty good though—he planted a string of churches there that you've heard of: Philippi, Thessalonica, Berea, Athens, Corinth. Worked out pretty good for us, too, since the gospel came from Europe to America.

God's "more"!

There was another trip on Paul's prayer list. He wanted to go to Rome. The answer to that prayer was delayed for years. While he waited, Paul wrote to his friends in Rome. Here, read some of the early lines of that letter:

> *I pray that I will be allowed to come to you ... I want very much to see you ... I want you to know that I planned many times to come to you, but have been prevented (Romans 1:10-13).*

Prevented? How come? Toward the end of the letter, he tells us:

> *It has always been my ambition to preach the gospel where Christ was not known ...* **This is why I have often been hindered from coming to you.** *But now that there is no more place for me to work in these regions, and since I have been longing for many years to see you, I plan to do so ... (Romans 15:20-24, emphasis mine).*

If Paul had whipped out his credit card and booked passage the first time he talked to his travel agent, that letter—the book of Romans, arguably history's greatest theological document—would never have been written.

There's still more of God's "more" in this story. When God finally answered Paul's prayer by getting him a ticket on a boat to Rome, it wasn't in a First Class cabin; it was in police custody. When he got to Rome he didn't go to church, he went to jail. Strange as it may seem, this was part of God's "more" answer to Paul's prayer, for he spent his two-year sentence teaching and writing letters. Copies of those letters are likely within reach of where you are sitting—to the Ephesians, the Philippians, the Colossians, and Philemon.

God's "more"!

God does immeasurably more than all we ask or imagine. Sometimes he skips minor revisions in favor of major rewrites. He may add a chapter here and there. Or toss the manuscript and start fresh.

You've heard the old saw about how God answers prayer: "sometimes he says yes, sometimes he says no, sometimes he says wait." We got that wrong. God doesn't say "no" to your prayers. When it seems that he does, wait and watch for his "more." He doesn't say "no," he says "more."

I wonder if there will be a place in heaven where God will display your prayers alongside his answers. If there is, I bet I'll see you standing there with your hands on your hips and a smile on your face, saying, "Whoa! So that's how that prayer worked out! I didn't think it had even been heard. Why that's immeasurably more than I asked for or imagined!"

Sharpen Your Faith

Here is a trio of attitudes you will do well to sharpen until they become habit.

> First, don't doubt God's power. It is unlimited. He is able to do more—immeasurably more—than you ask or imagine.

> Second, pray expectantly. When you ask according to his will, you can never ask for too much, and your expectations can never be too high.

> Third, don't get bent out of shape when it seems God isn't answering your prayer—keep an eye out for his "more."

Will he give you what you ask for?
That … or more.
You OK with that?

Summary Resolutions from Section Two

ASSURANCE

... (He) is able to do immeasurably more
than all we ask or imagine ...
—Ephesians 3:20

I RESOLVE to remember that God is in control.

I RESOLVE to remember that God isn't done with me—that I am a work in progress, not a finished product.

I RESOLVE to remember that I can be anything God wants me to be, and do anything God wants me to do.

I RESOLVE to remember that some things cannot be changed, and that some things can be: I will pray for grace to accept the first and courage to confront the second.

I RESOLVE to remember that there isn't a mile or a moment when I am alone.

I RESOLVE to remember that God is able to do more than all I ask or imagine.

SECTION THREE

COURAGE

Be strong and courageous!
Do not be afraid or discouraged.
For the Lord your God is with you wherever you go.
—JOSHUA 1:9 NLT

❧

*Do not fear, for I am with you; do not be dismayed, for I am
your God. I will strengthen you and help you (Isaiah 41:10).*

❧

"I 'll go in there for Dorothy. Wicked Witch or no Wicked Witch,
guards, or no guards, I'll tear them apart. I may not come out
alive, but I'm going in there. There's only one thing I want you
fellows to do."

"What's that?"

"Talk me out of it."

So spoke the Cowardly Lion in *The Wizard of Oz.* The Cowardly
Lion wanted courage.

Don't we all?

But how do we get it?

"You can't buy courage," wrote Peggy Noonan in an essay honoring
former President Ronald Reagan.

Not so fast, Peggy. I've found a couple of places where you can. For
somewhere around $100,000 a pop you can book former New York
mayor Rudolph Giuliani for a speech on courage. On a budget? Go for
Frank Miles, a Las Vegas performer. For just $10,000 Frank will juggle
and eat fire while making a speech on courage.

Then there's *The Courage Institute* that offers a menu of programs to
help you become the courageous person you've always wanted to be. For the
top of the line you'll have to pony up several thousand dollars. If you just
want a quick fix you might consider a one- or two-day workshop for $350 to
$500.

The problem is that high-dollar speakers fly in, speak up, and fly out.
If you opt for a seminar you fly in, listen up, and fly out.

I'm siding with Peggy on this one. Maybe a burst of bravado can be
bought in books, speeches, and seminars. But real courage? Probably not.

For that you need more than a temporary presence. And I think I know where you can get it ...

> *Be strong and courageous! Do not be afraid or discouraged. For the Lord your God is with you wherever you go (Joshua 1:9).*

11

AN INSIDE JOB

Since I am a runner, it caught my eye. An unusual full-page ad for a running shoe. Unusual because there wasn't a picture of the shoe. Or even a celebrity endorsement. It consisted of nothing but words. It gave the name of the shoe. Then, stretched across the page in large white letters on a solid-black background was just one word—*Courage!* Beneath it, this sentence: *Courage is doing what you're afraid to do.*

It was a come-on to convince me that owning that shoe would make me special, strong—courageous. Pretty smart advertising, actually—ramp up your courage for the price of a pair of shoes. I was smart enough to know what they were doing, but too smart to fall for it. (OK, so I swung by *Luke's Locker* running store and had a look. Even tried it on. You think bought it, don't you? Think what you want, I'm not saying.)

But I will tell you this: courage will cost you more than the price of a pair of shoes.

"Courage" wrote C.S. Lewis, "is not simply *one* of the virtues, but the form of every virtue at the testing point."

Winston Churchill agreed. He called courage "the first of human qualities...because it guarantees all the others."

Heroes

Liviu Librescu, was the son of Romanian Jewish parents. When his father was deported by the Nazis, Liviu was sent to a Soviet labor camp. He survived the Holocaust and was repatriated to Romania, where he continued his education. He eventually earned a PhD, only to be forced out of academia for his Israeli sympathies. In 1985 he and his wife came to the U.S., where he signed on as a professor of aerospace engineering.

On April 16, 2007, Dr. Librescu was teaching a class in Room 204 of Norris Hall Engineering Building on the Virginia Tech campus when Seung-Hui Cho entered the building and opened fire in a massacre that killed 32 people. When Cho attempted to enter Room 204, Dr. Librescu braced himself against the door and ordered his students to escape through the windows.

Cho's next blitz left the door in splinters and the professor dead.

Liviu Librescu gave his life to save his students.

Courage isn't usually that dramatic. Instead of a once-in-a-lifetime act of bravery, it is more often a relentless day-after-day demand.

Take Sherry Basu. When they pass out medals for bravery, Sherry deserves one. Barely over four feet tall, this twenty-four-year-old is sixty-five pounds of raw courage.

Sherry manages a one-day dry cleaner and laundry that adjoins the convenience store where I buy my morning paper and coffee. I try to time my trip to arrive at the same time Sherry does, so I can carry her purse and the plastic bag that contains her lunch. The first time I offered, she resisted—this tiny lady is inspiringly self-reliant.

Sherry has a congenital deformity that has her trapped in a twisted body with legs that won't work. Negotiating the five yards from the car to the front door of her business is an ordeal. Holding on to a railing she takes a short, faltering step with her left foot, then drags the right one alongside, then rests, then repeats the routine. Nothing in the shop is user-friendly for someone her size. The four steps from the customer service counter to the garment-conveyor carousel is a slow, torturous trip for Sherry. I would find it tough to live with her handicap for one day. She has lived with it every day of her life.

Sherry would be a shoo-in for disability benefits. Instead, she shows up for work six days a week and tackles a twelve hour shift, 7-to-7. I asked her what time she has to get up to get ready for work. Three-thirty, she said.

Never and always describe her: she *never* complains, and *always* smiles. *"Be strong and courageous!"* God said to Joshua. He doesn't need to say it to Sherry.

Liviu Librescu and Sherry Basu are examples of remarkable courage. Liviu's was a dramatic, one-time, lay-down-your-life act of bravery. Sherry's is a day-after-tedious-day treadmill of extraordinary valor. Both heroes.

Quiet Courage

It takes courage to risk life for a person or a cause.

It takes courage to get out of bed and go to work when your body fails you and depression assaults you.

Courage has many faces ...

> It is the single mom, struggling to make ends meet and hours stretch.
>
> It is the laid-off father, feeling the agony of hopelessness, but refusing to give up.
>
> It is the child of divorce, suffering the ache of rejection and battered self-image, but hanging in there.
>
> It is the caregiver, contending with exhaustion, but remaining compassionate and cheerful.
>
> It is the chemo patient, battling terror and fatigue, who jokes that bald is beautiful.
>
> It is the widow, facing old age alone, and the world with a smile.

And it is the person whose heartache is played out in the shadows, unknown to others. Your youthful dreams envisioned a lived-happily-ever-after adventure. But life may have taken a cruel turn and dumped you at a very different destination.

Daily. Quiet. Alone.

Without sympathy. Without praise. Without applause.

It's an Inside Job

Life is a mixture of joy and sorrow. You have good days and bad days. Victories and defeats. Times when you feel good, times when you don't.

What sets courageous people apart is that they refuse to give up. They stumble. Fall. Get up. Move on. The strongest aren't those who win, but those who don't quit when they lose.

> Courage doesn't always roar. Sometimes courage is the quiet voice at the end of the day saying, "I will try again tomorrow." —Mary Ann Radmacher

My friend Allen Isbell says that it is easier to control your actions than your attitudes. Bad attitudes, he says, are toxic. They poison from inside out. They contaminate relationships. Sabotage happiness. Make life miserable.

Reach deep within yourself and summon the courage to accept ownership of your attitude. Stop blaming others for your actions and attitudes, your flaws and failures. Someone hurt your feelings. Broke your heart. Shattered your dreams. Let it go! Move on. Forgive. However badly someone has treated you, and however deeply it hurts, get over it.

That's not easy, Joe.

I know.

Do it anyway. For your own sake. For until you do you will spend your days wallowing in the muck of self-pity and misery. So decide now, before you turn this page, to give up the blame game.

You can't change your life overnight, but you can change your direction this very minute. Your circumstances may be beyond your control, but your attitude isn't. Courage to change your attitude is an inside job.

Courage, my friend!

You are not alone. God offers three powerful promises:

> I will strengthen you;
> I will help you;
> I will uphold you.
>   (Isaiah 41:10).

Be strong and courageous!
Do not be afraid or discouraged.
For the Lord your God is with you wherever you go.

12

VICTORY IS JUST A DECISION AWAY

A t 4:35 p.m. on April 12, 1945, President Franklin Delano Roosevelt stopped breathing. The news stunned the nation and the world. Roosevelt had been president for over twelve years. Millions regarded him as indispensable to winning the war, and as the only American capable of dealing with leaders of other nations.

Vice President Truman was summoned to the White House. He arrived at 5:25 p.m. and was ushered into Eleanor Roosevelt's sitting room. "Harry," she said, "the President is dead." At 7:09 p.m. Harry S. Truman took the oath of office and became the 33rd President of the United States.

Hardly anyone outside of Washington knew who this man with the Missouri twang and thick glasses was. "The Hick from Missouri" some of his detractors called him. A failed haberdasher from Independence, Missouri, he had been vice president for only 82 days.

At that moment in history, foreign policy was the most important challenge facing the president. Truman knew next to nothing about foreign policy. Roosevelt hadn't included him in the loop: he had received zero briefing on the development of the atomic bomb, and hadn't so much as been introduced to Winston Churchill or Joseph Stalin.

Above all, Truman was not Franklin Delano Roosevelt—and most Americans could not imagine anyone else occupying the Oval Office. Roosevelt was adored by millions. Truman had none of his charismatic style.

Unknown. Untested. Yet now in charge of a full-scale war in Europe and the Pacific. It was a terrifying position to be in. In Berlin, an ecstatic

Joseph Goebbels telephoned Hitler with the "good news." This would be the turning point of the war, he exulted. Many feared the prediction would be accurate. So as Truman stepped into the White House, the world held its breath.

At another time, in another place, the transition of leadership was equally tense.

"Moses my servant is dead," God told Joshua.

Moses had been Israel's leader, not for twelve years, but for forty. No living Israelite—nor their parents before them—had known another leader. As frightening as it was for Truman to step into Roosevelt's shoes, it was more terrifying for Joshua to try to fill Moses' sandals. He took the oath of office following God's munificent eulogy of Moses: *"No one has ever shown the mighty power or performed the awesome deeds that Moses did."*

How would you like to try to follow that?!

Joshua was 85 years old, and God was drafting him to lead a rebellious, unmanageable bunch of malcontents into the Promised Land—a job that even Moses hadn't been able to pull off. It was a daunting assignment. Canaan was dotted with fortified cities and populated by giants. Joshua was commissioned to take them on with rag-tag troops that liked to fuss, but were afraid to fight.

There was a time when he would have tackled the task without giving it a second thought. He had been one of twelve spies sent to scout out Canaan—and one of only two with the guts to argue for attack. "With God on our side we'll have 'em for lunch!" he had said.[1]

But that was when he was young and in the ranks. Now that he was older and Commander in Chief he wasn't so sure. Be strong and courageous, God told him—and repeated it three times for emphasis.[2] He steeled him for action with a bouquet of promises:[3]

"No one will be able to stand up against you."
"I will never leave you nor forsake you."
"You will be prosperous and successful."
"The Lord your God will be with you wherever you go."

Meeting Your Crisis with Courage

You may be facing a "comparison" crisis of your own. Perhaps you're living in the shadow of a super successful father who expects you to live up to his star-quality performance. Or you may be married to a high-energy high-achiever, while, given a choice, you had rather take a nap than take a walk. Or possibly, like Truman, people unfairly compare you with a high-octane peer or predecessor.

Your crisis may be triggered by the discomfort of transitioning into unknown territory: a move to a new town, a new school, a new job, a new church, a new challenge. Or your scenery shift may be due to the breakup of your marriage, or the death of a loved one. It's uncomfortable to be in the old familiar places without the old familiar faces.

Change can be terrifying. But even in the face of fear you can possess courage.

John McCain spent five-and-a-half years in the "Hanoi Hilton" (Hoa Lo prison) in Vietnam, where beatings were routine, torture was commonplace, and fear was constant. "Fear," wrote McCain, "is indispensable to courage." For courage to be authentic he said, "it must encounter fear and prove itself superior to that fear."[4]

Love of his country is what gave McCain courage. Faith in your Father is what will give you courage.

That's what would have changed the picture for Israel. God didn't deliver them from slavery so they could slog 40 years in a desert of snakes and scorpions. He delivered them so they could live in a paradise of milk and honey. Early on Moses said, *"God has given you the land. Go up and take possession of it...Do not be afraid; do not be discouraged" (Deuteronomy 1:21).* Not yet, they said. First, let's send spies to have a look at the place; then let's vote. So the spies looked, and the people voted. The "no's" won by a lopsided 5-to-1 margin—a big win that was a huge loss. That vote cost the lives of 600,000 men who died in the desert when they could have lived in the Promised Land.

Don't make the same mistake. John McCain is right—you reach your Promised Land by facing your fear and proving yourself superior to it. That requires two things:

1. You have to let go of the past.

Moses was dead. That was a fact that Joshua had to accept.

Your past is dead. That is a fact that you have to accept. You may have been through some rough weather: divorce; failure; betrayal; death of a parent, companion, or child; or a discouraging church conflict. It's hard to bury a disappointing experience. But that's what you must do if you are to have a happy and productive future. That may mean you have to let go of some painful memory. It may mean that you have to forgive. Until you let go of the past you have no future!

2. You have to take the first step into the future.

When the Israelites skedaddled out of Egypt, the Red Sea separated them from freedom. God divided the waters and they crossed on dry ground.

Forty years later the Jordan River separated them from the Promised Land. No biggie for God. He's good at drying up rivers. But this time the crossing was conditional: *"Go stand in the river!"* God said.

Excuse me?

"Go stand in the river!"

Don't stay in camp and wait for a miracle. Pack up. Break camp. Move out. And don't stop at the river's edge and wait for God to work his magic. Go stand in the river.

You're kidding, right? At that time of year the Jordan was at flood-stage.

Guess what? The instant they set foot in the river it stopped flowing and piled up behind a God-made invisible dam. They walked across the impossible-to-cross Jordan on dry ground.[5]

What is it that's holding you back? Does the task seem too big? The problem too great? The habit too ingrained? The hurt too intense? The resentment too deep?

You don't have to win the whole battle on the first outing. Start small. Conquering the Promised Land seemed enormous: from the Euphrates River on the east to the Mediterranean Sea on the west; from the mountains of Lebanon on the north to the Nile River on the south. That seemed impossible—but stepping into the river didn't. And that's all they were asked to do to begin with.

Ask God for strength to take the next step. Just the next step. You don't have to look at the challenge of the next three months, or even the next three days. Only the next step. Just take that step. Then he will give you the strength to take the next one. And you're on your way!

It's frightening to give up a familiar past and step into an unfamiliar future. But until you do you don't have a future.

So, bury the past! You have a lot of life left to live. Every minute of it is in front of you—not a second of it behind you. God will provide a path through the river if you'll just take the first step.

Victory is just a decision away.

Listen to this advice and embrace this promise …

Be strong and courageous!
Do not be afraid or discouraged.
For the Lord your God is with you wherever you go.

13

FEED YOUR FAITH, NOT YOUR FEAR

"**M**r. Barnett, please get your belongings and come with me."

Puzzled, I followed her to the front of the plane, while people glared at me like I had a bomb in my briefcase.

"Here you go, Mr. Barnett, you're in seat 2A," said the perky flight attendant, flashing a mischievous smile.

"Uh ... there must be a mistake, ma'am. This is First Class. I have a Coach ticket."

"This is your lucky day," she said. "We have a full flight, so we're upgrading you to First Class."

My lucky day, indeed! I had arrived at the gate after everyone else had boarded, and got the last seat in Coach—middle seat, next-to-last row. There was already a carry-on under the seat in front of me. Even if I'd had a bad cold, which I didn't, I could have told you it was a diaper bag. Either that or the baby in my neighbor's lap was going bad.

First Class! Wow!

Dwight Moody said that you could go to heaven either first class or second class. His favorite Bible verse was, *"I will trust and not be afraid"* *(Isaiah 12:2).* That, he said, was going first class.

Trust ... and not be afraid!

Phobias from A to Z

Fredd Culbertson serves up a list of 537 phobias, trotting out our fears from A (ablutophobia) to Z (zoophobia).[1]

When I was a child my mother thought I had ablutophobia, fear of bathing, and lachanophobia, fear of vegetables. I definitely had aichmophobia, fear of needles, and ophidiophobia, fear of snakes. (Still have that one.)

I've never personally known anyone who had arachibutyrophobia, fear of peanut butter sticking to the roof of the mouth.

Here's my favorite: hippopotomonstrosesquippedaliophobia. Fear of long words.

Those who study such things say that there are four basic fears:

> Fear of Want
> Fear of Failure
> Fear of Suffering
> Fear of Death.

It's a quartet of storms that most encounter at some season of life. Let's have a look.

Fear of Want

Have you moved recently? I have, and I'm embarrassed. I found boxes that hadn't been unpacked since my last move, 25 years ago. For a quarter century I've gotten along just fine without these things that were had-to-haves when I bought them. So what did I do with them when the moving van backed up to my door this time? Most of them I gave away. A few of them I sold. And some of them I stored.

The next time I move I'll have to forage through these stored items and decide—again—what to do with them. For now they have a comfortable, if useless, home in climate-controlled storage.

These self-storage buildings that dot the landscape of my hometown would have baffled my grandfather. He couldn't have imagined a need for them. One hundred years ago, so I've read, the average American had 72 "wants," with sixteen of them rated "necessities." Today the average American has 484 "wants," with 94 of them considered "necessities." My grandpa's *want* list was shorter than my *got-to-have-it* list.

How about you? Let's take a stroll through your house and have a look in your closet, your jewelry box, your garage. Eyeball your appliances, your art work, your furniture. Oh, here you go, let's flip through that glossy catalogue on the coffee table, to the pages you've dog-eared—your want list. (I'm not picking on you—just trying to take the heat off of myself.)

Jesus said *"Life is not measured by how much one owns" (Luke 12:15 NCV)*. You'd never know it by taking a peek at our possessions would you? But he was right of course. If you measure your worth by what you own, you are not the owner, you are the owned.

And it won't be long until every last bit of it belongs to someone else. That was Jesus' point in a story he told about a man whose life was consumed in beefing up his stash. *"You fool!"* God said. (It's the only time God ever called a man a fool.) *"You fool! Tonight you will die. Then who will get what you have stored up?" (Luke 12:20 CEV)*.

Paul's words are unsettling: *"We should be satisfied just to have food and clothes" (1 Timothy 6:8)*. There are two ways to be rich. One is to have many assets. The other is to have few wants.

Fear of want grows out of wanting too much. Or wanting the wrong things.

Fear of Failure

Why this gut-gripping fear of failure? Because you want to be accepted, admired, approved, and appreciated. And failure wilts those flowers.

You look at others—whose success you magnify and whose failure you minimize—and compare your performance to theirs. They've soared. You've fizzled.

Stop it! Just stop it! Comparing your achievements to those of others is not only pointless, it's poisonous. Don't do it anymore.

The main cause of fear of failure is past mess-ups.

Instead of finishing school, you dropped out.
Instead of climbing to the top, you stalled out at average.

Instead of building a good marriage, you got a divorce.
Instead of being the perfect parent, you fouled up.

That ship has sailed. Give it up! You can't sweep up the trash of past mistakes anymore than you can unscramble an egg. So you messed up. Knowing what you know now, you would do a better job if you had another shot at it. But you didn't know then what you know now, and you don't have another shot at it. So stop looking in the rearview mirror. You have zero control over the past.

You're not the first to goof up, you know. Noah got drunk. Moses got mad. David got aroused. Peter got scared.

That was a whale of a stormy night when Peter messed up and denied Jesus. He was facing into vicious winds—one nail-biting experience after another. He could easily have gone over the edge and ended up like Judas. Why didn't he? Because he had come-back courage.

And think about this! Judas could have weathered his storm and been among the greatest success stories in the Bible ... if he had had the courage to try again.

The difference between the loser and the winner is that the loser accepts failure as final; the winner doesn't!

Afraid if you try again you'll fail again? By not trying again you guarantee it. Get up, dust off and have another go at it. *"We ... don't give up and quit ... We get knocked down, but we get up again and keep going ... we never give up (2 Corinthians 4:8-9, 16 TLB).*

Fear of Suffering

Scary word, suffering. It raises questions:

When suffering strikes will I be weak, or strong?
Will I become better, or turn bitter?
Will my faith stay steady, or get shaky?

We don't know the answer to those questions. What we do know is that suffering is certain—an unavoidable storm. You're going to lose a parent, or a child, or a mate. There is going to be loss, illness, sorrow.

And, barring an early exit, you're going to grow old. The demands for repairs on the house you live in increase—no sooner do you get one body part fixed than another malfunctions. A lopsided percentage of senior hours is spent in physician's offices. I chuckled at the response of the caregiver who knits while she waits for her clients to wrap up their doctor visits. The receptionist, seeing an afghan she had just finished, asked her how long it took to do it. "Two physicals, one bone density scan, and one colonoscopy," she replied.

Even so, I cast my vote in favor of aging. Age has its advantages. And youth is not all it's cracked up to be. Morrie Schwartz nailed it:

> ... *the young are not wise. They have very little understanding about life. ... people are manipulating you, telling you to buy this perfume and you'll be beautiful, or this pair of jeans and you'll be sexy—and you believe them! It's such nonsense.*[2]

> *As you grow, you learn more. If you stayed at twenty-two, you'd always be as ignorant as you were at twenty-two. Aging is not just decay, you know. It's growth.*[3]

The body wears out, yes, but the spirit grows stronger. "*Our physical body is becoming older and weaker, but our spirit inside us is made new every day*" (2 Corinthians 4:16 NCV). Suffering afflicts only the physical part of us. And it's only temporary.

> *These troubles and sufferings of ours are, after all, quite small and won't last very long. ... The troubles will soon be over, but the joys to come will last forever* (2 Corinthians 4:17-18 TLB).

Don't forget that a "hurrah" day is coming, when God will take away every fear and wipe away every tear (Revelation 21:4).

Fear of Death

Death! Our archenemy. Our unavoidable appointment. Our fiercest and final storm. Our greatest fear.

Sooner than we think the Final Act of our earthly drama will play out. The last song will be sung. The maestro will lay down his baton. The curtain will fall ... and there will be no curtain call.

The thought of death is unnerving. *"The terrors of death have fallen upon me. Fear and trembling come upon me, and horror overwhelms me" (Psalm 55:4-5).*

Death is the great equalizer. It treats rich and poor the same. Psalm 49 doesn't pull any punches about the short-lived glory of earthly fame and fortune. May I paraphrase its points?

> *All the money in the world can't buy immunity from death (7-9).*

> *Both the wise and the foolish will die and leave their wealth to others (10).*

> *The rich may have a fat portfolio. A business, building, or street may be named for them. But the day will come when they will move out of their opulent digs and into a three-by-six-foot plot, just like everyone else (11, 14).*

> *Don't be overly impressed with the rich and famous; they won't take a dime with them when they die (16-17).*

> *Though men praise you when you prosper and applaud you when you achieve, the kudos die soon, and so do you (18-19).*

Now for the good news!

Die we must. But not alone, not in fear, and not forever. Those who know next to nothing about the Bible know this verse: *"Even though I walk through the valley of the shadow of death, I will fear no evil, for you are with me" (Psalm 23:4).*

By dying and rising Jesus set us free from fear; emancipated *"those who all their lives were held in slavery by their fear of death" (Hebrews 2:14-15).* *"Because I live,"* he promised, *"you also will live" (John 14:19).*

Feed Your Faith, Not Your Fear

Well, there they are, a quartet of hurricane-force storms:

> Fear of Want.
> Fear of Failure.
> Fear of Suffering.
> Fear of Death.

Can you survive them? You bet! Feed your faith and your fear will starve. Dip into your survival supplies and pull out this canister of nonperishable faith-feeding snacks:

> *The Lord is my light and my salvation—whom shall I fear? The Lord is the stronghold of my life—of whom shall I be afraid? (Psalm 27:1).*

> *In God I trust; I will not be afraid. (Psalm 56:4).*

> *Do not fear, for I am with you; do not be dismayed, for I am your God. I will strengthen you and help you; I will uphold you … (Isaiah 41:10).*

> *Peace I leave with you; my peace I give you. … Do not let your hearts be troubled and do not be afraid (John 14:27).*

*God has said, "Never will I leave you; never will I forsake you." So **we** say with confidence, "The Lord is my helper; I will not be afraid" (Hebrews 13:5-6, emphasis mine).*

Be strong and courageous!
Do not be afraid or discouraged.
For the Lord your God is with you wherever you go.

14

TODAY YOU FIGHT ... AND WIN

Discouragement! It may be Satan's deadliest weapon!

Conquering Canaan wasn't the challenge. Conquering discouragement was the challenge. Canaan was populated by the Amorites, Perizzites, Canaanites, Hittites, Girgashites, Hivites, and Jebusites—seven nations, all stronger than Israel. Not a problem. God would see to that. These foes, strong as they were, couldn't defeat Joshua. But there was one enemy that might: discouragement. So God told Joshua, *"Do not be afraid or discouraged."*

How, pray tell, do you pull that off?

I think I know someone that can tell you.[1]

His job this morning was to go check on his brothers, deliver their lunch of bread and cheese, then report back to his dad on how they were doing.

He had just arrived at their camp when he heard a roar and saw soldiers scatter.

It was the loudest voice he'd ever heard: *"I defy the ranks of Israel! Give me a man and let us fight each other."*

"Who is that?!" he asked.

"It's the giant from Gath," said a nervous recruit. "He has the whole army spooked."

"You gotta be kidding! Who is this uncircumcised Philistine that he should defy the armies of the living God?"

It had been going on for over a month now. Eighty times—every morning and every evening for 40 days—Goliath had strutted into the valley and shouted his challenge: *"Give me a man and let us fight each other."* And every time Goliath shouted Saul's soldiers ran.

"Your worries are over," David said, "I'll take care of him."

"Get real, boy! Wait 'til you see the size of this dude. He's over nine feet tall. His armor weighs more than you."

David wasn't listening. He was already on the move. Stooping at the edge of a stream, he pocketed five rocks and headed into the valley. Goliath saw him coming, and cursed with rage. "A boy?! They sent a boy to fight me? C'mere, peach fuzz. I'm gonna feed you to the birds and beasts."

A chipmunk pitted against a rhino.

Wide-eyed, open-mouthed soldiers watched as puffs of dust swirled where David's sandals hit the ground as he ran toward the giant while seating a stone in the pocket of his sling. Now he was the one shouting:

> *You come against me with a sword and spear and javelin,
> but I come against you in the name of the Lord Almighty, the
> God of the armies of Israel, whom you have defied. This is
> the day the Lord will hand you over to me, and I'll strike you
> down and cut off your head.*

Well, you know the story. David cleaned Goliath's clock with one rock, and lopped off his head with his own sword.

Dealing with Discouragement

Satan knew that Goliath was no match for David. It would take more than a nine-foot behemoth wearing 125 pounds of armor to whip this kid. Goliath had a sword, a javelin, and a spear with a shaft as thick as a fence post. That wasn't enough to put David down. Satan knew that. The only weapon in Satan's arsenal that had a chance at doing this boy in was *discouragement,* and he started wielding it before David ever heard of Goliath.

Beginning at home.

David's dad wasn't "Father of the Year" quality. He didn't attend David's sling-shot competitions, much less his harp recitals. He didn't even show up when David won the blue ribbon at the County Fair Sheep Show. He acted as if David didn't exist—except when it came to assigning family chores.

The day came when God had had enough of King Saul. Fed up with his foul disposition and rebellious ways, he told Samuel, *"I am sending you to Jesse of Bethlehem. I have chosen one of his sons to be king."*

When Samuel saw Eliab, Jesse's number one son, he was impressed. He had the size and the looks—an excellent choice to replace King Saul. *"Surely the Lord's anointed stands here,"* Samuel thought. "Wrong!" God said.

So Jesse called in his number two son, Abinadab. *"The Lord has not chosen this one either,"* Samuel told him.

Shammah perhaps? No, not Shammah.

One-by-one they came. And one-by-one they were rejected. Seven of them!

"Are these all the sons you have?" asked Samuel. "Well ... there's the runt, David. But he's out tending the sheep." Jesse hadn't even invited his youngest son to the party. *"Send for him,"* Samuel ordered; *"we will not sit down until he arrives."* So Jesse sent a servant to fetch the runt, and they waited. Smelling of sheep the puzzled boy came through the door. "He's the one," God told Samuel. "Anoint him."

You'd think Jesse would have been popping his buttons: "That's my boy!" You'd think he would have been collaring his friends: "Can you keep a secret? This has to be on the QT for awhile. My boy David has been named next King. Whatcha think of that?!"

But that's not what happened. Jesse didn't even lighten David's chores when he became King-in-waiting. Just kept him busy taking care of the sheep—when he didn't have him running errands, that is.

Three of David's older brothers were in the army, camped in the Valley of Elah, where Goliath was spouting off. Jesse called David in from sheep-keeping to carry lunch to his brothers and bring back news from them.

It's hard to imagine anything more discouraging than having a parent that doesn't give a hoot about you. Always putting you down instead of lifting you up. Always wanting you to be something different than what you are ...

> Dad wanted an all-state fullback; instead, he got a son who wanted to play the violin.
>
> Mom wanted a homecoming queen; instead she got a daughter who wanted to dissect bugs.
>
> Grades? Never high enough.
> Performance? Never good enough.
> Dress? Never classy enough.
> Looks? Never swank enough.

Every boy and girl needs parental affirmation. Something David never got from his dad.

Nor from his brothers. His oldest sibling Eliab was a hunk, but he wasn't about to go man-to-man with Goliath. And he resented his baby brother's brass. When he saw him fraternizing with the soldiers and asking questions about Goliath, he exploded: *"Why aren't you minding your own business, tending that scrawny flock of sheep?"* He wrote him off as a cocky brat with a big mouth, who didn't belong out here with real men.

Judging by David's response it wasn't the first time big brother had put him down. *"Now what have I done?"* he asked. *"Can't I even ask a question?"*

Then there was King Saul, desperate for someone to take on the foul-mouthed giant. Taking Goliath out was so critical that Saul had come up with a three-part reward-package for anyone who would do it:

1) a huge cash advance;
2) his daughter's hand in marriage;
3) lifetime exemption from taxes.

"I'm your man," said David.

You would think Saul would be ecstatic that finally someone was willing to step up to the plate. Instead, he brushed David off with this discouraging put down: *"You are not able to go out against this Philistine and fight him; you are only a boy ..."*

Well, that boy fought that Philistine, if it could be called a fight. In the first fifteen seconds of the first round, he dropped the champion, saving Saul and Israel from embarrassing defeat.

The nation was grateful. Ticker-tape parade. Women dancing in the streets, beating their tambourines, and singing at the top of their voices ...

> *Saul has slain his thousands,*
> *and David his tens of thousands.*

Instead of being grateful, Saul was galled. The kudos the people dished out to David sent Saul into a jealous rage that lasted until the day he died.

People idolize their war heroes. Presidents don't get Ticker-tape parades. The guys who ride in the open-tops and wave at adoring crowds are the MacArthurs, the Eisenhowers, the Schwarzkopfs.

King Saul couldn't handle that.

David served Saul faithfully. Brought him repeated victories. Still, Saul hunted him with maniacal vengeance. Sent assassins to his house, and deployed soldiers by the thousands to chase him down and kill him—even joining the hunt himself now and then.

Twice, while Saul was leading the death-to-David posse, David— unknown to Saul—was close enough to kill him with a single sword thrust. Twice he refused to end the life of the man who was bent on ending his. And twice Saul rewarded him by trying to pin him to the wall with a spear.

How discouraging!

David couldn't seem to do anything right. He wasn't good enough for his family. And was too good for his King.

The first names of David's detractors were Jesse, Eliab, Saul, and Goliath. But they all had the same last name: *Discouragement.*

Your number one enemy wears the same surname as David's: *Discouragement.* What is his first name? Could it be one of these?

Anger
Resentment
Lust
Envy
Addiction
Habit
Temper
Tongue

Maybe your Goliath's name is on that list. Maybe not. But you know his name. Yes, you know the name of the giant that has been controlling you. Haunting you. Taunting you—shouting, "You're a weakling; you can't win this fight!" Convincing you that the battle is hopelessly lost.

No more! This is the day you put a stop to it. This is the day you march into your Valley of Elah and take on your giant. This is the day you claim the power and presence of God, running toward your giant with a shout: *"I come against you in the name of the Lord Almighty! ... the battle is the Lord's!"*

This is the day you fight ... and win!

Be strong and courageous!
Do not be afraid or discouraged.
For the Lord your God is with you wherever you go.

15

EVEN THERE

On the south edge of Huntsville, Texas, just an hour from my front door, stands a dazzling, eye-watering statue of Sam Houston. It is the world's tallest statue of an American hero— 77 feet high. You can see "Big Sam" for miles—60 tons of concrete and steel.

Impressive! But it can't hold a candle to the statue King Nebuchadnezzar raised on the plain of Dura in Babylon. Neb's statue trumped Sam's in both size and materials. His was 90-feet-tall, besting Sam's by 13 feet. Concrete and steel? Nah, Neb's statue was gold!

People stop by the side of the road to gawk at Sam. They look up, but they don't bow down. They stare, but they don't worship.

That wouldn't work for King Nebuchadnezzar. When he finished his statue he threw a doozy of a dedication ceremony.[1]

> He ordered all the important leaders in the province, everybody who was anybody, to the dedication ceremony of the statue. They all came for the dedication, all the important people, and took their places before the statue that Nebuchadnezzar had erected.
>
> A herald then proclaimed in a loud voice: "Attention, everyone! Every race, color, and creed, listen! When you hear the band strike up—all the trumpets and trombones, the tubas and baritones, the drums and cymbals—fall to your knees and worship the gold statue that King Nebuchadnezzar has set up. Anyone who does not kneel and worship shall be thrown immediately into a roaring furnace" (Daniel 3:2-6 MSG).

Three Hebrew teens—Shadrach, Meshach, and Abednego—had been brought to Babylon as captives after Nebuchadnezzar besieged Jerusalem. They were brighter and more gifted than anyone in Nebuchadnezzar's kingdom, and rose quickly to positions of power and leadership because God was with them. They served the king faithfully, but drew the line at bending the knee to his statue. A gaggle of Jew-haters tattled to the king, and he was furious! He summoned the three and gave them a good dressing down.

> *"I'm giving you a second chance—but from now on, when the big band strikes up you must go to your knees and worship the statue I have made. If you don't worship it, you will be pitched into a roaring furnace, no questions asked. Who is the god who can rescue you from my power?" (Daniel 3:14-15 MSG).*

Their answer?

> *"If we are thrown into the blazing furnace, the God we serve is able to save us from it … But even if he does not, we want you to know, O king, that we will not serve your gods or worship the image of gold you have set up" (Daniel 3:17-18).*

That did it!

In a rage he gave the order to stoke the furnace: make it seven times hotter than usual, he commanded. Up went the heat, and in went Shadrach, Meshach, and Abednego.

As the entourage watched, the king counted …

"One, two, three—*four!*"

Nebuchadnezzar rubbed his eyes, then counted again.

"One, two, three—*four!*"

"Didn't we throw three men into the furnace?" he asked.

"Yes," they said, *"we did indeed, Your Majesty."*

"Well, look!" Nebuchadnezzar shouted. *"I see* **four** *men, unbound, walking around in the fire, and they aren't even hurt by the flames! And the fourth looks like a god!"*

Then Nebuchadnezzar came as close as he could to the open door of the flaming furnace and yelled: "Shadrach, Meshach, and Abednego ... Come out! Come here!" So they stepped out of the fire.

Then the princes, governors, captains, and counselors crowded around them and saw that the fire hadn't touched them—not a hair of their heads was singed; their coats were unscorched, and they didn't even smell of smoke!

"One, two, three—*four!"* the king counted. *"And the fourth looks like a god!"*

On November 21, 1915, Sir Ernest Shackleton's ship, *Endurance,* sank near Elephant Island off the coast of Antarctica. Shackleton took his two strongest men, Frank Worsley and Tom Crean, and set sail in an open boat to get help for their twenty marooned comrades. They battled the stormy sea for more than 800 miles. When they landed they were still 22 miles from help. For 36 hours they crawled over the perilous peaks and glassy glaciers of South Georgia before reaching the Stromness whaling station.

Wherever Shackleton told the story of that treacherous trip, people sucked in their breath. It was an iron-hearted act of bravery; a mission of incredible endurance. But Sir Ernest didn't considered it heroic. He spoke rather of his consciousness of a divine companion. At a banquet in his honor in London he said, "We all felt that there were, not three, but *four* of us."

"One, two, three—*four!*"

Sir Ernest never spoke of the experience without quoting the text that fed his courage:

> *If I take the wings of the morning, and dwell in the uttermost parts of the sea, even there shall Thy hand lead me and Thy right hand shall hold me (Psalm 139:9-10).*

Shadrach, Meshach, and Abednego had courage—because they had firm faith in the presence of God.

Sir Ernest Shackleton had courage—because he had firm faith in the presence of God.

Strength, courage, banishment of fear, and elimination of discouragement rest on that foundation—firm faith in the presence of God.

God sealed Joshua's commission to lead Israel with three sentences.

> The first sentence consisted of two positive directives: *Be strong and courageous.*

> The second sentence consisted of two negative directives: *Do not be afraid or discouraged.*

> The third sentence consisted of one promise: *The Lord your God is with you wherever you go.*

The first two sentences hinge on the third. Strength and courage, and elimination of fear and discouragement, come from a single source: firm faith in the presence of God.

When Moses said goodbye to Israel, these were his words:

> *Be strong and courageous. Do not be afraid or terrified ... for the Lord your God goes with you; he will never leave you nor forsake you (Deuteronomy 31:6).*

When he passed the mantle of leadership to Joshua, these were his words:

> *Be strong and courageous … The Lord himself goes before you and will be with you; he will never leave you nor forsake you. Do not be afraid; do not be discouraged (Deuteronomy 31:7-8).*

When God finalized Joshua's commission, these were his words:

> *I will never leave you nor forsake you. … Be strong and courageous! Do not be afraid or discouraged. For the Lord your God is with you wherever you go (Joshua 1:5, 9).*

You can't help but notice the similarity of the words. There is a good reason: the key to courage is firm faith in the presence of God.

Israel fell short of that faith, and as a result fell short of courage. The fallout was disastrous: forty years of desert wanderings, and the wilderness deaths of over a million people.

Things haven't changed much. Sunday's pews are occupied by thousands who have almost no Monday-thru-Saturday feeling of the presence of God. They sing, pray, commune—then leave the sanctuary, picking up the life they left outside the door. A life dominated by worry and fear. A life without strength or courage. A life of defeat and discouragement.

Courage is an uncommon quality because a sense of God's presence is an uncommon quality.

The Lord your God is with you wherever you go. The question is not do you know these words? The question is do you believe them?

Have one more look at Sir Ernest Shackleton's favorite text:

> *If I take the wings of the morning, and dwell in the uttermost parts of the sea, **even there** shall Thy hand lead me*

and Thy right hand shall hold me (Psalm 139:9-10 emphasis mine).

Take note of those two words, *"even there!"*

He is with you *wherever* you go! When you wonder if that *wherever* includes the painful wind-shifts in your life the answer is *even there.*

When my marriage falls apart? *Even there!*

When someone dear to me causes excruciating heartache? *Even there!*

When circumstances seem hopeless? *Even there!*

When death snatches my dearest on earth? *Even there!*

When old age diminishes me? *Even there!*

You are never alone. His companionship is *wherever* and *forever.*

Be strong and courageous!
Do not be afraid or discouraged.
For the Lord your God is with you wherever you go.

Summary Resolutions from Section Three

COURAGE

Be strong and courageous!
Do not be afraid or discouraged.
For the Lord your God is with you wherever you go.
—Joshua 1:9 NLT

I RESOLVE that no matter how difficult today may be I will have the courage to try again tomorrow.

I RESOLVE to control my attitude as well as my action.

I RESOLVE to live by the words never and always: *never* complain; *always* smile.

I RESOLVE to live in the awareness that all of life I have left is in front of me, none of it behind me.

I RESOLVE to feed my faith, not my fear.

I RESOLVE to remember that God's companionship is wherever and forever.

SECTION FOUR

PATIENCE

Wait for the Lord;
be strong and take heart
and wait for the Lord.
—PSALM 27:14 NIV

Those who wait for the Lord will gain new strength; They will mount up with wings like eagles, They will run and not get tired, They will walk and not become weary (Isaiah 40:31 NASB).

❧

"When I wrote *Simple Abundance*," said best selling author Sarah Ban Breathnach, "it was turned down 30 times before I got a publisher. Looking back, if it had been published earlier it never would have struck a chord, but later people were ready to listen to the message. Isn't divine timing amazing?"

Yes, it is Sarah. But it's a hard lesson to learn.

The interval between prayer and its answer sometimes seems long. *"Why must the godly wait for him in vain?"* asked Job (Job 24:1). *"I cry out to you, O God, but you do not answer,"* he complained (Job 30:20).

Why doesn't he answer? Why doesn't he act?

He does. When the time is right. And only he knows when that is.

Until then we have to wait.

If you're in a storm that seems like it may last forever, head for the closet where you store your storm-supplies and start digging for *Patience*. It's probably close to the bottom of the box, because it isn't used very often. It's found in the cancer ward more often than the corner office. It's rarely seen in CEOs or politicians, not to mention authors.

You won't survive life's storms without it, so make sure you have a good supply on hand.

Wait for the Lord;
be strong and take heart
and wait for the Lord.

16

THE WAITING ROOM

I'm not the best-qualified person to write about patience. I get restless at a fast-food restaurant when the wait time edges toward three minutes.

And I don't have a friendly relationship with automated phone systems. Is there anything less user-friendly? Anything that more conclusively proves that the customer does *not* come first? Not that I can think of. These days help is a half-hour of button-punches away—interspersed with promotional messages and elevator music as I race toward the completion of my life cycle.

"Your call is important to us," I am assured.

"Calls are answered in the order in which they are received," I am told.

"Please don't hang up. The next available operator will take your call," I am promised.

I'm quivering in anticipation.

Have you heard about the man who called the phone company and dutifully punched in the extension listed on his phone bill? The next thing he heard was a recording that said: "You have reached the right department on the first try. This is against company policy. Please hang up and try again."

Patience. Let's talk about it.

What is the worst storm you've ever been in?

I've been in four that carved a notch in my memory: two tornadoes and two snowstorms.

The tornadoes were scary, but short-lived.

One of the snowstorms was an eye-watering Colorado blizzard that trapped me in a ten-hour white-knuckle drive. If it was ten percent as bad as the stories I've told about it, it was one of the worst storms in history.

But the worst storm I've ever been in was not the worst storm I've ever been in. (Yes, that is what I meant to say.) It wasn't life-threatening. I was in a comfortable house, with food, water, and electricity. Still, it was the worst storm I've ever been in—a whiteout that had me holed up for five days that seemed like five months.

It's not that I was alone. I wasn't. I was with my good buddy and his wife. That was the problem! I would have traded my accommodation under their roof for a cell in a monastery.

It's amazing how time changes people. My friend had changed a lot since I'd last seen him—10 days ago. He wasn't nearly as funny now as he had been a week and a half before. Nor as intelligent. Humph! What a dimwit! In politics and religion he had become an unreasonable, unteachable, opinionated jerk. His personality had become prickly and he was sooo easily irritated. How could I ever have been close to such a schmuck?!

And his wife? Let's not even go there.

I wasn't getting much sleep, even though I was hitting the sack earlier than I ever had. I kept getting up and looking out the window. It was like living inside a snow globe that someone kept turning upside down.

After the first night the snow was up to the wheel wells on my car. The next morning it was up to the hood. The third morning my car had disappeared! It became apparent that even if I could get out of the house I couldn't get out of town. It was torture to realize that I would be spending the rest of my life in that house with that surly, sulky, crabby, cranky couple. The temperature outside was warm compared to my sub-zero mood.

We didn't run out of food. We didn't run out of water. We didn't run out of books. What we ran out of was patience.

When you have to wait too long for a storm to clear you'd rather be anywhere than where you are, with anyone than who you are with.

It takes *Trust* to survive storms. And *Assurance*. And *Courage*. Those are survival supplies we've talked about in the first three sections of this book. But as important as they are, none of the three will be effective without *Patience*.

Yet, *Patience* probably isn't on your list when you think of surviving life's storms. It seems admirable, but not essential. It appears weak compared to these other qualities. It doesn't have the ruggedness of *Trust* or the boldness of *Assurance* or the muscle of *Courage*. But be warned, you're not likely to survive your storm without it. In fact, you're not likely to hang on to trust, assurance, or courage without it.

Loss of patience almost sunk John the Baptist. From his prison cell he dispatched his disciples to ask Jesus a question: *"Are you the one who is to come, or are we to wait for another?" (Matthew 11:3)*. Underline that word *wait*. John was tired of waiting.

He was discouraged. And why not? He was accustomed to the wide-open spaces of the country. City life didn't work for John, much less prison life. But you know John well enough to know that he could tough out prison. What he couldn't handle was Jesus' pace. Why was he moving so slowly? Why didn't he assert himself? John's patience was wearing thin.

Grab a word, any word you wish, to describe John. I don't know what word you'll choose, but I know one that you won't: *Quiet*. John was anything but quiet, and Jesus was being way too quiet to suit him. From the day John started preaching *"The kingdom of heaven is near,"* and pointing to Jesus as *"The Lamb of God, who takes away the sin of the world,"* he wanted to get on with it. Waiting didn't fit his personality or his plan.

Some Bible scholars think it was lack of patience that did Judas in—that his betrayal was an effort to force Jesus to come out in the open and declare himself the Messiah. He had been waiting three years. It was time for action!

After Jesus' resurrection he spent his final 40 days on earth talking to his disciples about the kingdom. Do you detect a hint of frustration when they asked him, *"Lord, are you at this time going to restore the kingdom to Israel?"* His answer had to be the last thing that these weary-of-waiting men wanted to hear: *"It is not for you to know the times or dates the Father has set" (Acts 1:6-7).* Aw, c'mon!

That wasn't the first time their patience was tried by waiting for him to act. There was a night when they got pounded by a teeth-jarring storm on the Sea of Galilee. He had agreed to join them, but night came, the storm struck, and John tells us that *"Jesus had not yet come to them" (John 6:17 NRSV).*

Where was he? Why was he waiting so long?

I know the answer to the first question, but not to the second. I know where he was—he was on the mountain praying. But I don't know why he was waiting so long to join them.

Was he unaware of the storm? Unconcerned about their concern? No. From his perch on the mountain he was watching them as they fought for their lives: *"He saw that they were in serious trouble, rowing hard and struggling against the wind and waves" (Mark 6:48 TLB).* And when the time was right he came calmly walking across the water: *"'Take courage.' he said. 'Don't be afraid.' Then he climbed into the boat with them, and the wind died down" (Mark 6:50-51).*

Make no mistake, he is aware of the storm that's hammering you.

> When your night is dark, he is watching.
> When your sea is rough, he is watching.
> When you're in serious trouble, he is watching.

So why hasn't he yet come to you? I don't know. But he will. When the time is right he will climb into your boat, and the storm will stop.

Waiting for his coming is tough; nerve-racking.

"The most difficult discipline in the Christian life, in my opinion," said Charles Swindoll, "is waiting."

I agree.

My wife spent 15 years dying with progressive multiple sclerosis. I spent quite a bit of time during those years in hospital waiting rooms. If you have been there you know that it gives new meaning to the word "wait."

I wrote part of this chapter in the surgical waiting room at University Medical Center. Everyone in that room was waiting for their own private storm to subside. Every few minutes a doctor in surgical garb walked into the room and called a family name. An individual—or sometimes an entire family—stepped forward. I watched as they listened to the doctor, and asked questions. Some punched a hole in the air with their fist and blurted out an exuberant "Yesss!" when the doctor explained the patient's condition. Others grabbed for an available arm or piece of furniture to keep their knees from buckling. Some smiled. Others wept.

I was especially impressed with one doctor. She was articulate and sensitive. Her explanation of the surgery was clear and her demeanor reassuring. "We've done everything we can do," she said. "Now we just have to wait for God to work."

She was right, you know. We do everything we can do, whatever the situation—then we have to wait for God to finish the job.

Sometimes it seems that he walks slowly. He has his reasons. So be patient. Let him set the pace.

That's not easy. As I confessed earlier, patience isn't my long suit. But I learned a few things about waiting for God's answer to prayer during the years of my wife's illness. I prayed that he would give her comfort and make her well. I haven't a single doubt that he answered my prayer, although not according to my kindergarten level of understanding. I'm confident that she is comfortable. And well.

Patience is a tough tool to master. Proficient use is an acquired skill. If you become an accomplished user you will be one-in-a-million—and you will survive any storm.

Wait for the Lord;
be strong and take heart
and wait for the Lord.

17

ANYTHING BUT THAT!

I know the first thing you did this morning.

"No you don't," you say.

"Bet I do."

"Okay, wise guy, what? Made my bed?"

"No."

"Brushed my teeth?"

"No."

"Took a shower?"

"No."

"Dressed?"

"No."

"Ate breakfast?"

"No."

"What, then?"

"You looked at the clock. That's the first thing you did this morning."

It's also the last thing you did before you went to bed last night. And it's what you did when you woke up during the night. You looked at the clock.

And you've done it a jillion times since you got up.

Why? You already know how long it takes you to shower, shave, blow-dry, dress, eat breakfast. You've clicked off these routines thousands of times. Still, you keep an eye on the clock while you do them, to make sure you're on time.

You know what time you have to walk out the door in order to be where you have to be on time. And how long your daily commute takes. But you keep glancing at your car clock to make sure you're on time.

You know how long it takes to walk from your parking space to your workplace, but you keep squinting at your watch to be certain you're on time.

You know how long it takes to get to the restaurant, cafeteria, or deli where you have lunch. How long you have to stand in line. How long it takes to eat. To pay. And to get back to your workplace. But you keep peeking at your watch to be sure you're on time.

You know how long it takes at the end of the day to put your stuff away, clear your space, exit the building, and get to your car. And how long it takes to drive home. But you keep checking the dashboard clock to see if you are on time.

There is an irresistible itch to watch the clock, to know that you're on time.

Between the two of us, you and I probably have enough clocks to stock a clock shop.

Follow me here; see if your inventory matches mine.

In the lower right hand corner of my computer screen there is a small clock.

There's a clock on my printer, one on my telephone, and one on my cell phone.

There is a large wall clock across from my desk that my eye is repeatedly drawn to.

In my kitchen there is a clock on my microwave, another on my oven, and one on the wall.

In my bedroom there's a clock on my dresser, and one on my night table.

There is a clock in my bathroom.

And one in my utility room.

There is a clock on the dashboard of my car. And another one on my GPS screen.

And on my left wrist there is a watch.

Does that pretty well match your collection?

I have breakfast, lunch, and dinner when the clock tells me it's time—whether I'm hungry or not. I am controlled by the clock! It isn't my servant, it is my master, cracking the whip to make sure I am where I am supposed to be when I am supposed to be there, doing what I am supposed to be doing when I am supposed to be doing it. As Thoreau said, we have become the "tools of our tools."

Measuring Worth by Productivity

Do you know who invented the clock? You may want to choke a monk when you find out. The mechanical clock was developed by Benedictine monks in the 12th and 13th centuries to bring precise order to their seven daily periods of devotion.

By the middle of the 14th century that monastery clock had been hijacked by commerce to bring regimentation to the workplace. Fixed working hours and measurable production became the norm. A worker's worth was judged by how much he produced in a specified period of time. Worth has largely been weighed on that scale ever since.

The haunting question is: What do you have to show for your time? That's why some projects—writing a book, for instance—zap self-esteem. There have been times while working on this manuscript that things have moved briskly: thoughts have come easily, words have flowed smoothly, and I have come to the end of the day feeling I have used my time well— *I have been productive.* Then *whap!*—days have dragged by with little measurable progress. On those days even a well-meaning inquiry like "How's the book coming?" is unnerving. It chides me for my meager output.

We get antsy when we can't see concrete results, because we measure our worth by our productivity.

Productive Tools

How right Thoreau was: we have become the "tools of our tools." That is far truer now than when he said it.

The computer that sits on your desk or in your lap is a powerful tool that promises to help you get more done in less time—pledges to serve you faithfully. You take the bait, and as soon as the first cable is plugged into the first port you become its slave.

I, like most of my generation, had to be pulled kicking and screaming into the computer age. But now the first thing I do in the morning (after looking at the clock, of course) is turn on my computer, and the last thing I do at night is turn it off. My computer is my most constant companion. (How pitiful is that?!)

I was notified this morning that the server my computer is connected to will be shut down for 30 minutes at 3:30 this afternoon. I've been watching the clock and scheduling everything around that half-hour interruption ever since.

My computer has totally changed the way I work. Without leaving my keyboard to browse my bookshelves or visit my local library, I have a repository of dictionaries, commentaries, encyclopedias, lexicons, concordances, topical Bibles, word studies, maps, hymns, and over 20 Bible translations—plus internet access to scads of information on almost any subject.

Even though my computer puts all of this information at my fingertips, it never runs fast enough. I bought a new one because my old one was too slow. This one was so screamin' fast I had to have it. "It won't be long until you'll think it is slow," said my technician. It has already happened. (Sigh.) It has a rotten attitude; gets sluggish and snotty for no reason. I hate that!

It pulled the ultimate snippy stunt while I was writing this chapter: it went into a coma—totally shut down. *Kaput!* I called my technician, confident he would guide me through a few mouse-clicks and I would be up-and-running in no time. He asked a few questions, then said, "I hope you had everything backed up, because you've crashed." I seesawed between sweats and chills, freaking out about days of work and pages of manuscript lost out there ... wherever that lost stuff goes. *Pfft! Poof!*

I nearly had a stroke when he told me to pack it up and send it to him. What?! Couldn't he walk me through the process and fix it over the phone? Nope, not this time. He might as well have pulled the plug on my life-support. I overnighted it to him—guaranteed delivery by 10 o'clock the next morning. (How long would that have taken a couple of generations ago?) He promised to resuscitate it and overnight it back to me. I would be without it for one day and thin slices of two more—36 hours at most. I spent most of those hours scribbling illegible words on a yellow pad—aiming anxious glances at the space where my computer usually sits, while it was 600 miles away undergoing major surgery. I was pretty sure it would recover before I did. The pain was excruciating.

You find it amusing that this happened to me while I was writing about patience don't you? You are a very sick person!

We're in a Hurry

We don't mess around! We toss back the covers and hit the ground running!

We wolf our instant oatmeal, and gulp our instant coffee while scanning the morning paper. My paper of choice runs 64 pages on an average day. No problem: page two dishes up a 16-column-inch block dubbed *News in 90 Seconds.* Sixty-four pages condensed to a minute-and-a-half. Can't beat that!

Then, out the door.

After a day at full throttle we race back to the house—making brief stops to grab a few bucks at the ATM, fill our tank at the pay-at-the-pump island, slosh through the three-minute car wash, and pick up our clothes at the *In-by-9-Out-by-5* cleaners.

For dinner we scarf a pre-packaged microwaved entrée, topped off with a pouch of instant pudding. (Calvin—of *Calvin and Hobbes*—studied the instructions on a microwave dinner box. "It takes six minutes to microwave this," he groused. "Who's got time for that?")

After dinner, what? Spend time with the kids? Are you kidding? They haven't been seen in months—they call from the bedroom on their cell phone to avoid the long trip to the TV room for face-to-face conversation. That's okay with us—we don't have the patience for a face-to-face. Impatience destroys our relationships with people.

And with God. His timing doesn't measure up to our expectations; his response to our prayers is too long in coming.

Phillips Brooks was known for his calm disposition. A friend who dropped by was surprised to see the preacher feverishly pacing the floor. "What's the trouble?" he asked. "The trouble is," replied Brooks, "that I'm in a hurry, but God isn't."

I know the feeling, don't you?

"Father, I need some help here!" I pray.

"Wait! says God.

"Please, Lord," I yelp, "anything but that!"

Patience is the fine art of learning to wait until God is ready to act.

Here's a sampling of the Bible's "wait" verses. Try them on for size. I think you'll find one that fits.

> *Be patient and wait for the Lord to act... (Psalm 37:7 TEV).*

> *I wait quietly before God, for my hope is in him (Psalm 62:5 NLT).*

> *Wait for the Lord, and he will deliver you (Proverbs 20:22).*

Blessed are all those who wait for him to help them (Isaiah 30:18 TLB).

Those who wait for the Lord will gain new strength; They will mount up with wings like eagles, They will run and not get tired, They will walk and not become weary (Isaiah 40:31 NASB).

For since the world began no one has seen or heard of such a God as ours, who works for those who wait for him! (Isaiah 64:4 TLB).

The Lord is good to those who wait for him... (Lamentations 3:25 NRSV).

Wait for your God, and don't give up on him—ever! (Hosea:12:6 MSG).

And then there's our theme text ...

> *Wait for the Lord;*
> *be strong and take heart*
> *and wait for the Lord.*

18

IN THE MEANTIME

He was on solitary duty in the Holy of Holies. The flickering light from the golden candlestick cast eerie shadows. The aroma of incense swirled about him. He was lost in thought. Suddenly an angel tapped him on the shoulder and said, "Zechariah …"

"Yeeoowww! You scared the daylights outa me!" Zechariah screamed.

"Sorry about that," said the angel. "I just dropped by to tell you that your prayer has been heard—your wife Elizabeth is going to have a baby, a boy."

Yeah, right!

They had prayed for a son. Desperately! Fervently! Pleadingly! Constantly! But that was a long time ago, when they were young and hopeful. They had long since given up on an answer to that prayer.

So with fire in his eyes and hands on his hips Zechariah faced off with angel Gabriel. "Verrry funny! I'm an old man, and you don't have to have 20/20 to see that the Mrs. has a bumper crop of liver spots. Look! You're not supposed to be in here, and I'm busy. I don't have time for your sick jokes!"

"This is no joke, Zechariah. God sent me to tell you that your prayer has been heard. When the time is right you're going to have a son."[1]

When the time is right!

When Zechariah and Elizabeth had prayed for a son the time wasn't right. God wasn't ignoring their request; he was just waiting for the right time to grant it. And was it ever worth the wait! They named him John. And what a son he was:[2]

> A joy and delight to his parents.
> Great in the sight of the Lord.

Filled with the Holy Spirit.
Bringing many people back to the Lord.
Preparing the way for the coming of Jesus.
And this tip-of-the-hat from Jesus himself: *"among those born of women there is no one greater than John"* *(Luke 7:28).*

Zechariah and Elizabeth learned that good things come to those who wait—learned that Psalm 27:14 is a good text to hang on to: *"Wait for the Lord; be strong and take heart and wait for the Lord."*

Look at the first four words of that sentence: *Wait for the Lord.*

Now, look at the last four words: *wait for the Lord.*

In between those two "waits" is what we are advised to do in the meantime: *be strong and take heart.*

Good advice! Because *in the meantime* experiences are notorious for torrential rains and high winds that will turn your umbrella inside out and blow your hat off.

The apostle Paul had lived in storm country long enough. He wanted a transfer: *"I want to leave this life and be with Christ,"* he wrote (Philippians 1:23 NCV).

"Not yet," God said.

So Paul waited.

In the meantime the storms he faced—listed in 2 Corinthians 11—leave us shaking our heads:

He was frequently in prison.
Beaten up more times than he could count.
Constantly stalked by death.
He was stoned once.
Flogged eight times.
Shipwrecked three times.
He was in constant danger ...
      from robbers.

from Jews.

from Gentiles.

from false Christians.

from mobs in the cities.

from death in the deserts.

He was exhausted, wracked with pain, and unable to sleep.

He was often hungry and thirsty.

And miserably cold.

Heartbreaking, spirit-sapping storms didn't end with the first century. The twenty-first has its share. Just ask Nita Short. She will introduce you to some people she met during her chaplaincy at the Texas Medical Center in Houston—people who know firsthand how tough things can get *in the meantime.*

A mother who sat day after day caring for her brain-damaged daughter who couldn't move or talk.

A young man who was terrified of needles, but gave blood so that his father could live.

A young lady who had been diagnosed with multiple sclerosis—who, instead of giving in to self-pity, came to the hospital each day to encourage other MS patients.

A wife who sat day after day, week after week—hollow-eyed from lack of sleep—watching her husband suffer the torture of cancer treatment.

An old man with no living relatives to give comfort, who braved his pain alone.

I'm sure that you too know people who are leaning into the winds of *in the meantime* ordeals—people like these friends of mine:

A businessman who is facing a crushing financial crisis and the probability of embarrassing bankruptcy.

A woman who is struggling to survive the procedures of an unwanted—and very nasty—divorce.

A man who is trapped in a miserable marriage.

A mom and dad whose child has broken their hearts.

A husband and father who is trying to endure with dignity the final stages of an excruciating battle with cancer.

Maybe your name belongs on this list too. You've been slammed by storms that you didn't see coming and that you don't understand. Where is God? you wonder. Why doesn't he do something? You want the agony to end—want a "lived-happily-ever-after" life. Living in a storm that refuses to let up is non-stop misery.

You've heard upbeat bromides like "be strong" and "take heart" until you're ready to snap. Advice is easier to swallow if it comes from someone who has been there, so maybe a page from Paul's journal is the ticket:

> *We are perplexed because we don't know why things happen as they do, but we don't give up and quit...We get knocked down, but we get up again and keep going...we never give up (2 Corinthians 4:8-9, 16 TLB).*

Those last three words are worth underlining …

Never Give Up

You've prayed ... and prayed ... and prayed. Urgently. Earnestly. Pleadingly. For all the good it's done you might as well have saved your breath. There has been no answer. Zero! Zilch! So you've given up—stopped believing that your prayer will be answered.

You're in good company: Zechariah gave up too. He didn't stop worshipping and serving God, but he stopped believing that his prayer for a son would be answered.

But was he ever in for a surprise! "Your prayer has been heard," Gabriel told him. Zechariah was young when he prayed for a son to play catch with. Now he was old. But God hadn't thrown out his prayer and scratched him off his list because his faith faltered.

> God isn't going to yank your prayer from his in-box because you quit believing.

> He isn't going to trash your request because you quit praying.

> He isn't going to give up on you because you give up on him.

He has heard your prayer, and at the right time he will answer. *In the meantime* he is *waiting on you* to learn to *wait on him.*

Delay does not mean denial.

Presently unanswered does not mean permanently ungranted.

Your prayer will be answered. Today? Maybe, maybe not. Tomorrow? Maybe, maybe not. But one day.

The timing may be in question, but the answer isn't. Even when you are discouraged by the delay don't doubt the promise: *"We can trust God to keep his promise"* (Hebrews 10:23 TEV).

God—because he sees the big picture—knows when to send answers to your prayers, and when to delay them. Trust him. Be grateful when he answers. Be patient when he delays. It pleases us when he is quick to answer. It pleases him when we trust him even when he delays. It is human to want to see before believing. It is Spirit-led to believe before seeing: *"Blessed are those who have not seen and yet have believed"* *(John 20:29).*

His answer will come ... in exactly the right way at exactly the right time.

No peace equals the peace of being at peace with God's timetable — being content, even delighted, for him to respond to your needs at the time and in the way that he chooses.

Be patient. His timing is perfect.

Pray this prayer with me:

> Dear God, I ask you to give me grace to wait patiently
> until it pleases you to answer my prayer.
> For I believe you will do it
> in your own time and in your own way. Amen.

> *Wait for the Lord;*
> *be strong and take heart*
> *and wait for the Lord.*

19

I OUGHT TO …

The headline didn't do much for me: *Keys to Unlocking Gridlock's Potential.* But the subtitle drew me in: *Turn that traffic jam into an opportunity to firm those abs, boost antioxidant intake, examine career goals or listen to a book.*

The column ticked off a list of things that will whip you into shape when you're stuck in traffic: breathing techniques; behind-the-wheel calisthenics; facial exercises (I have a hunch these will signal "road rage" to the guy in the next lane); snacks to amp up your antioxidant intake; and audio books to juice up your self-image.

Pretty good stuff, because traffic congestion causes our blood pressure to shoot up, our ulcers to act up, and our temper to flare up. We're wired for action. Waiting in line or in traffic triggers agitation.

You won't have to reach far back in memory to recall when you were on the verge of coming unhinged. Your stomach was churning and you were mad enough to bite the lid off a tin can, because someone was inconsiderate of your schedule, your importance.

> You got stuck in a slow-moving check-out line at the grocery store. *Move it! I don't have all day!*

> The driver ahead of you didn't gun it the second the light turned green. *Hello! It ain't gonna get any greener!*

> Your spouse was late—again. *My time means nothing to her!*

That's our high-octane world for you. We're in a hurry.

Waiting is harder than working. At the beginning of a project there is the thrill of the start, the excitement of the launch. At the end there is the thrill of the finish, the glow and glory of the accomplishment. But between the beginning and the end there are stale stretches of plodding and waiting that turn the mood blue.

The trick is to find a way to stay positive during the down times—the wait times. What should you do while you wait?

Sometimes the best thing you can do is just wait—quietly, prayerfully, submissively: *"Be patient and wait for the Lord to act" (Psalm 37:7 TEV).*

But wait time doesn't necessarily have to be defined by apathy, tedium, and drift. It can be a time of meaning and purpose, action and hope.

I Ought to …

"What kind of people ought you to be?" asked Peter (2 Peter 3:11). Oswald Chambers said, "Every call comes with an *'ought'* behind it."

Pesky word, *ought:* You *ought* to do this! You *ought* to do that!

One way to deal with an *ought* is to numb the conscience so that the prodding is no longer felt. But the only proper response to an *ought* is action.

How long has it been since you had a serious look at some of your *oughts*? Does anything in this list touch a nerve?

I ought to write that letter.
I ought to make that phone call.
I ought to apologize.
I ought to control my temper.
I ought to change my attitude.
I ought to stop complaining.
I ought to forget the past.

I ought to forgive.
I ought to give him/her the benefit of the doubt.
I ought to encourage others more.
I ought to stop gossiping.
I ought to listen more and talk less.
I ought to give up that habit.
I ought to stop blaming others for my problems.
I ought to stop making excuses.
I ought to be kinder.
I ought to be more understanding.
I ought to be more considerate.
I ought to be more tolerant.
I ought to be more agreeable.
I ought to be more patient.
I ought to be more helpful.
I ought to be more optimistic.
I ought to be more pleasant.
I ought to be more grateful.
I ought to be more generous.
I ought to quit being so grouchy.
I ought to quit being so touchy.
I ought to quit being so critical.
I ought to quit being so judgmental.
I ought to quit being so argumentative.
I ought quit being such a know-it-all.

Do you see anything in that list that you ought to do? If you do—and I'm pretty sure that you do—I suggest that you bookmark this page, lay this book aside and do that thing. We rarely get around to doing what we delay, so stop right now and do the *I ought to* thing that's tugging at you. Not tomorrow. Now!

Just Begin

Hmmm. I'm getting vibes that you didn't follow the advice of the last paragraph. I'm not quite ready to let you off the hook, so let me give it another shot.

The main reason you don't do what you *ought to* is because you don't *want to.* If the *want to* is there, with God's help you can do it. In fact, he will even help you want to: *"God is working in you to help you want to do and be able to do what pleases him (Philippians 2:13 NCV).*

You have identified something that you ought to do, right? But you haven't done it yet. Why? Is it too big? Too much to swallow? Okay, don't swallow the whole thing, just take a small bite out of it? For the moment, don't commit to finishing, only to beginning.

Let me show you, by taking a few *ought to* items from our list:

I ought to write that letter. Don't wait until you have the whole letter mapped out. Just address the envelope and take a stab at the first paragraph.

I ought to apologize. Don't think yet about everything you need to say. Just set a specific time to do it (next Tuesday, or whenever). And decide if you will do it face-to-face, by phone, or by letter.

I ought to be more agreeable. Don't go for a total personality makeover. Just commit to this one small step: the next time you are about to create a fuss, stop and ask yourself if the issue is important enough to fight over; important enough to sour a relationship.

I ought to be more pleasant. Do nothing more than pick a specific day, and commit to being cheerful and gracious in every contact for that one day.

You get the idea. Just begin. It will take you farther than you imagine.

Dr. Wayne W. Dyer says that the secret to getting his writing completed on schedule is that "each and every day, at a prescribed time, regardless of how many interruptions I have or reasons for doing something else, I begin the next essay. I don't vow to complete it, only to begin. And lo and behold ... once I have begun the reading, research, and actual writing of the opening sentence, I find that the work just manages to get completed."[1]

Here on my desk is a book by F.W. Boreham, *A Bunch of Everlastings.* On my breakfast table is another Boreham book, *A Handful of Stars.* And on my night table is yet another, *Ships of Pearl.* I have 38 of the 48 books Boreham wrote. They have provided me many hours of delightful reading, stimulated my thoughts, and given me fresh insights.

Boreham's first book was published in 1912; his last in 1961. Most of them are out of print, but their influence still lives. His pulpit ministry was limited to New Zealand and Australia, but his writing ministry was worldwide. Billy Graham once introduced him as "the man whose illustrations are in all our sermons."

How did he turn out such voluminous prose? By beginning. He was often frustrated by some thought that teased him, but wouldn't jell. Then one day he would pick up his pen and begin to play with the idea, and—voilà!—the thoughts came, the words flowed, and soon the piece was done.

C.S. Lewis, arguably the most famous and prolific apologist of the twentieth century did the same. Over and over he put pen to paper to begin a letter, essay, or book. Lewis died on November 22, 1963—the same day John F. Kennedy was assassinated—but over 60 of his books remain in print, and more of his books are sold today than those of any Christian writer in history.

These two men—Boreham and Lewis—both confessed that the most difficult part of writing was beginning. But begin they did. And finish they did. They were patient at their craft, and their writings continue to bless the world.

Hesitancy to begin is what keeps you from being as productive as you wish to be. You put it off and push it back, and before you know it the day is gone.

What is it that you need to do, intend to do? Maybe it's something from the *"I ought to"* list—maybe something else. Refuse to accept the excuses you have used to explain why you haven't done it. The main reason you haven't completed it is that you haven't begun it.

So while you wait for the Lord, be strong and take heart. Today that may mean, while you wait … do something!

Wait for the Lord;
be strong and take heart
and wait for the Lord.

20

THE RACE OF YOUR LIFE

On May 6, 1954, a 25-year-old Englishman raced through cold crosswinds on a muddy track in a race that propelled him into fame.

On the 50th anniversary of that race, May 6, 2004, newspapers around the world displayed the black-and-white photo that captured the moment. It showed Roger Bannister, head tilted back, mouth open gasping for air, and legs mud-splattered as they carried him to the first sub-four-minute mile in history. Three minutes, 59.4 seconds, to be exact. In those days, a four-minute mile was considered unreachable by most track and field experts.

Bannister, a gaunt 6-1, 150 pound medical student had been tormented for two years by his disappointing performance at the 1952 Olympics in Helsinki. He had expected—and was heavily favored—to win the gold medal in the mile. The Duke of Edinburgh even made the trip to the Games to witness the triumph. But Bannister was never in contention that day. He finished a bitterly disappointing fourth.

He had planned to win the gold at the Olympics, and then abandon racing to pursue his medical studies. But after the loss he knew he couldn't quit until he put the polish back on his reputation, and there was no better way to do that than to be the first to break the four-minute mile. It would be like Lindbergh crossing the Atlantic or Peary reaching the North Pole. He would do whatever it took to reach that goal.

Bannister's accomplishment ranks among the most significant in the history of sports, because like Babe Ruth hitting 60 home runs in one season, or Wilt Chamberlain scoring 100 points in one game, only one person can be the first. A new world-record has been set 18 times since

Bannister's feat. Over 2,000 runners have clocked a sub-four-minute mile since he did it. But he was the first. It was a spectacular performance.

This gritty Brit's determination was impressive—putting med-school on hold for two years; refusing to listen to those who said he was reaching for an impossible goal; fighting through discouragement and a skeptical press. Being persistent. And patient.

Patience doesn't rank very high on our list of virtues. It lacks glamour and muscle. The very word has a ring of monotony. We view it with a yawn. Halford Luccock called it the "ho-hum" virtue.

John Chrysostom, on the other hand, called patience "the queen of virtues."

You've seen its opposite—impatience—in many places:

In the doctor's waiting room, where an "impatient patient" snapped at the receptionist and stomped out of the office.

In the guy who lost his cool waiting in line at the service station and raced out of the lot, tires smoking and screeching.

In the grocery store where an agitated lady blew a fuse because someone stepped in line ahead of her.

In the department store where a woman with red-face and shrill-voice ripped into a new employee who was having trouble ringing up the sale.

There's an old saying that runs this way: "All things come to him who waits." Patience is the quality that makes waiting possible. It keeps you at the task when you are tempted to quit.

Impatience, on the other hand, tempts you to do one of two things: give up, or compromise.

Give Up

When you face the fierce winds of impatience the inclination is to give up, to bail out.

I don't have to put up with a surly boss, unreasonable hours, and back-stabbing co-workers. Color me gone!

Making this marriage work is way harder than I expected. I'm outa here!

When I tackled this challenge (pursuing an advanced degree, learning a second language, losing weight, writing a book), it seemed like a good idea. But it's too hard. I'm giving it up.

You'll never get anywhere if you ditch a two year project in two weeks. Resist the temptation to give up too quickly.

Patience is a fruit of the Spirit (Galatians 5:22) and, like any fruit, it ripens at its own pace. My father was in his 98th year when he said, "I know I'm not very patient, but with the good Lord's help I'm going to get there." He was still working on it at 98. For most of us development of patience is a work-in-progress that lasts a lifetime.

Fruit ripens slowly. Things change slowly. Wounds heal slowly. Impatience doesn't accelerate the ripening process or the healing process by a single hour. As Shakespeare said, "How poor are they who have not patience! What wound did ever heal but by degree?"

Be patient. Don't give up.

> *Let us not become weary in doing good, for at the proper time we will reap a harvest if we do not give up (Galatians 6:9).*

Compromise

If you succeed in resisting the temptation to give up, impatience attacks on a second front: it tempts you to compromise—to plot cagey maneuvers to reach your goals; to devise detours to get to your desired destination.

That's what Abraham and Sarah did. God had promised that they would have a son. But the years passed, they grew old, and the promise seemed increasingly improbable. So Sarah hatched a plan of her own. *"The Lord has kept me from having children,"* she said to Abraham. *"Go, sleep with my maidservant; perhaps I can build a family through her" (Genesis 16:2).* So that's what he did—with miserable results all the way around.

The kingdom of Judah made the same mistake. For 150 years Assyria had been expanding by swallowing neighbor nations. Now they were flexing their muscles and threatening Judah. God sent Isaiah to assure Judah of his protection. Not good enough! The danger was too close; the chance of success too small. So they cooked up their own plan: they dashed down to Egypt and cut a deal with Pharaoh for protection.

God wasn't pleased.

> *"Woe to the obstinate children,"* declares the Lord, *"to those who carry out plans that are not mine, forming an alliance, but not by my Spirit, heaping sin upon sin; who go down to Egypt without consulting me; who look for help to Pharaoh's protection, to Egypt's shade for refuge" (Isaiah 30:1-2).*

God warned them that they were headed for a train wreck:

> *"Pharaoh's protection will be to your shame, Egypt's shade will bring you disgrace" (Isaiah 30:3).*

> *"Woe to those who go down to Egypt for help ... but do not look to the Holy One of Israel, or seek help from the Lord. ... the Egyptians are men and not God ... " (Isaiah 31:1, 3).*

Impatience will backfire on you. Designing your own plan and charging ahead without consulting God will bring grief rather than glory.

What should Judah have done? And what should you do when you feel boxed in by obstacles and frustrations? Here is the answer:

"Only in returning to me and waiting for me will you be saved. In quietness and confidence is your strength. ... Blessed are those who wait for him to help them" (Isaiah 30:15, 18 NLT).

Here are two more sentences from the prophet that are worth storing with your storm supplies:

No one who waits for my help will be disappointed (Isaiah 49:23 TEV).

(God) acts on behalf of those who wait for him (Isaiah 64:4).

The Race of Your Life

The achievement of Roger Bannister was thrilling. Still, in the big picture I doubt that running a sub-four-minute mile—even the first one—is all that important.

But the race you're running is!

Paul ran the same race, and he thought it was the only one worth running:

"I consider my life worth nothing to me, if only I may finish the race and complete the task the Lord Jesus has given me," (Acts 20:24).

"Run in such a way as to get the prize," he urged. *"Everyone who competes in the games goes into strict training. They do it to get a crown that will not last; but we do it to get a crown that will last forever"* (1 Corinthians 9:24-25).

You're in the race of your life. You're closer to the finish line than you've ever been, and getting closer with every step. It'll be over before you know it.

> *Let us run with patience the race that is set before us.*
> *—Hebrews 12:1 ASV*

Summary Resolutions from Section Four

PATIENCE

Wait for the Lord;
be strong and take heart
and wait for the Lord.
—Psalm 27:14

I RESOLVE to be patient and pleasant with the people God puts in my path.

I RESOLVE to "be patient and wait for the Lord to act" (Psalm 37:7).

I RESOLVE to patiently wait for God to answer my prayers at whatever time and in whatever way he chooses.

I RESOLVE to remember that delay is not denial.

I RESOLVE to take the first step, no matter how small, realizing that I can never finish what I have never started.

I RESOLVE to run with patience the race that God has given me to run (Hebrews 12:1).

SECTION FIVE

PEACE

Let him have all your worries and cares,
for he is always thinking about you and
watching everything that concerns you.
—1 PETER 5:7 TLB

What kind of man is this? Even the winds and the waves obey him! (Matthew 8:27).

❧

A t the end of Thornton Wilder's *Our Town* Emily dies while giving birth. She is given permission to go back once more— invisibly—to her hometown of Grover's Corners. There she sees her mother making breakfast. And Howie the milkman. And constable Warren. And Papa.

Lamenting how fast life passes, and how the living are consumed by trivial matters, she again takes her leave. "Good-by world. Good-by Grover's Corners ... Mama and Papa. Good-by to clocks ticking ... and Mama's sunflowers. And food and coffee. And new-ironed dresses and hot baths ... and sleeping and waking up. Oh, earth, you're too wonderful for anybody to realize you. Do any human beings ever realize life while they live it?—every, every minute?"

At the cemetery she speaks to her long-dead mother-in-law: "Oh, Mother Gibbs, I never realized before how troubled and how ... how in the dark live persons are. ... From morning till night, that's all they are— troubled."[1]

Yes, unless they embrace the peace that Jesus offers. It isn't an offer of exemption from storms, but a promise of peace in the midst of storms— an inner peace that all the forces of the world or of hell can't take from you.

When the winds of tragedy blow, the sleet of disappointment stings, the waves of grief surge, and everything seems to be spinning apart, it isn't. He is in control of those storms that seem so threatening: *"Even the winds and the waves obey him!"*

Into the dark room of your life, where you have retreated because you are afraid, anxious, discouraged, remorseful, conscience-stricken, or alienated, he comes and opens the curtains, letting in the light with a simple, but so profound, promise: *"My peace I give you."*

21

LET HIM CARRY YOUR STUFF

"Big Don" had a last name, but he didn't need one—everybody knew "Big Don."

As you've probably guessed, he was a mountain of a man—6-6, 350 pounds when he was behaving at the table. A lot more than that when he wasn't.

I loved the big guy. He was on my staff as youth minister. A treasured friend, a confidant.

And he carried my stuff! That's one of the reasons I loved him, because he carried my stuff.

Back in the days when they let you haul as much luggage onto an airplane as you could handle, I never checked any bags. I wrestled all of them onboard, even if it meant enlisting the help of a fellow passenger. Changing planes and negotiating concourses of crowded airports was a challenge. By the time I got home from a trip I was bushed.

"Big Don" was always at the airport to meet me, although that wasn't in his job description. At 5-10, 150 pounds, I was dragging bags that weighed more than I did. As I stumbled through the jetway, I would spot "Big Don," laughing and slapping his substantial leg.

The moment I cleared the gate he was there. "Here brother, let me carry those for you!" he'd say. He would grab every piece of my baggage, and without breaking a sweat off he'd trot through the airport and across the parking lot, lugging the load that had worn me out.

He did the same thing in our work relationship. How he did it I'll never know, but he always showed up at exactly the right time. I would have a committee meeting to attend, a speech to make, a counseling session to fulfill, a sermon to prepare—none of which was any more important or time-consuming than the entries in his own Day Planner. Seeing some chore that he could take off my hands he'd say, "Let me do that for you." Whatever the hour, day or night, my big friend was there to help.

You don't encounter many people like that in a lifetime, and it's one of life's great blessings when you do.

(Just in case you're curious, it's Williams. That's his last name—"Big Don" Williams.)

I hope there is someone in your life like "Big Don." Someone who shares your burdens. Someone who is concerned about your concerns. Someone who carries your stuff.

Even if you don't have a flesh-and-blood friend like that, God wants to step up and lighten your load. Seeing you buckle under your burden of worries and cares he says, "Let me carry that for you!"

Peter said it this way: *"Let him have all your worries and cares."*

"Every evening I turn my worries over to God," said Mary Crowley. "He's going to be up all night anyway."

Victor Hugo said something similar: "Go to sleep in peace. God is awake."

Have you heard about the woman who suffered serious sleep deprivation because of her fear of burglars? One night she heard a noise, shook her husband awake, and sent him to investigate. He had been through the drill many times—but this time he came nose-to-nose with a real live burglar. Unfazed, he said to the intruder, "Good evening, I'm pleased to see you. Come upstairs and meet my wife. She's been expecting you for ten years."

God wants to take on your worries and cares. Little ones and big ones; trivial ones and tragic ones. None is too small to escape his concern, and none too large for him to handle.

Peter cast a wide net: *"Let him have all your worries and cares."* See that *all*? *All* your worries and cares.

This isn't bumper sticker theology. It's a heavenly offer! God isn't playing games with you; he wants to lift your load, carry your stuff. And will if you'll let him.

Here's the way Paul said it:

> *Do not be anxious about anything, but in everything, by prayer and petition, with thanksgiving, present your requests to God. And the peace of God, which transcends all understanding, will guard your hearts and your minds in Christ Jesus (Philippians 4:6-7).*

THE LIVING BIBLE translates that first phrase: "Don't worry about *anything.*"

Instead, we worry about *everything:*

> war, terrorism, crime, road rage, and global warming …
> the economy, social security, jobs, taxes, and identity theft …
> politicians, bribes, and earmarks …
> country, community, school, and church …
> spouse, parents, children, grandchildren, and friends …
> World Series, Super Bowls, and NBA finals …
> fat, wrinkles, wattle, cellulite, and liver spots …
> bad hair, gray hair, and no hair …
> health, aging, and dying.

We worry that the worst that can happen will happen: the sore throat is probably esophageal cancer; the stomach spasm is a sure signal of colon cancer; the raging headache, a brain tumor no doubt.

We worry because people don't act the way we think they should. Don't toe the party line. Don't drive in the right lane. Don't treat us right. Don't eat with the right fork. Don't see things the way we do.

We even worry about things in the distant future. Like the woman who went to a lecture where the speaker ranted that the universe was going to self-destruct in five billion years; whereupon the dear lady fainted. When she came to she was asked why she was so upset about something that was five billion years away. Heaving a sigh of relief she said, "Oh thank God, I thought he said five *million* years."

Paul advised us to stop carrying all that baggage. His recipe consisted of three steps:

> Don't worry about *anything*.
> Pray about *everything*.
> Think about *these things*.

Don't worry about anything? How do you pull that off? By praying about everything, and thinking about the right things.

And he adds that our prayers should be seasoned with thanksgiving. It's difficult to worry and be thankful at the same time. Give this a try: list some things for which you are thankful—and try to put a price tag on them.

> What price would you put on your health? $_____
> Your eyesight? $_____
> Your family? $_____
> Your friends? $_____

You get the idea. Worry won't find a welcome in the heart of the thankful.

Anne Lamott said that she has two main prayers: *"Help me, help me, help me"* and *"Thank you, thank you, thank you."* Petition and thanksgiving. A good formula.

All this worrying about the future is sloppy thinking. It keeps you from enjoying the present. One way to overcome worry is to consciously focus your thinking on present blessings: good family, good friends, good job, good church, good books, good health, good appetite, good food, good teeth. (Make your own list.)

When you put your heart into thinking about such blessings worry seems obscene.

That's why Paul added these words:

> *... whatever is true, whatever is noble, whatever is right, whatever is pure, whatever is lovely, whatever is admirable ... think about such things (Philippians 4: 8).*

Unless you are unusually gifted at multitasking you can't worry when you're thinking about what is true, noble, right, pure, lovely, and admirable.

So there you have Paul's perfect defense against the stiff winds of worry ...

> Don't worry about *anything*.
> Pray about *everything*.
> Think about the *right things*.

Are you trying to carry too much stuff? Too many worries and cares? A strong, loving God is ready to lift that load. Let him carry your stuff.

> *Let him have all your worries and cares,*
> *for he is always thinking about you and*
> *watching everything that concerns you.*

22

YOU AND BILL GATES

S
ir Cecil Rhodes was co-founder of the De Beers Mining Company. In 1902, De Beers controlled 90% of the world's diamonds, making Rhodes one of the richest men in the world. An interviewer, alluding to his wealth, said, "You must be a very happy man." "Happy?" Sir Cecil replied, "Good Lord, no! I have spent my life making money. Now I'm having to spend half of it on doctors to keep me out of the grave and the other half on lawyers to keep me out of jail."

Money and worry go hand-in-hand. Those who have it worry about it as much as those who don't; and those who don't as much as those who do.

Jesus hit it head-on:

You cannot serve both God and Money.

Therefore I tell you, do not worry about your life, what you will eat or drink; or about your body, what you will wear. Is not life more important than food, and the body more important than clothes? Look at the birds of the air; they do not sow or reap or store away in barns, and yet your heavenly Father feeds them. Are you not much more valuable than they? Who of you by worrying can add a single hour to his life?

And why do you worry about clothes? See how the lilies of the field grow. They do not labor or spin. Yet I tell you that not even Solomon in all his splendor was dressed like one of these. If that is how God clothes the grass of the field, which is here today and tomorrow is thrown into the fire, will he not much

151

more clothe you, O you of little faith? So do not worry, saying, "What shall we eat?" or "What shall we drink?" or "What shall we wear?" For the pagans run after all these things, and your heavenly Father knows that you need them. But seek first his kingdom and his righteousness, and all these things will be given to you as well. Therefore do not worry about tomorrow, for tomorrow will worry about itself. Each day has enough trouble of its own (Matthew 6:24-34).

It would be hard to miss the message:

Worry is ungodly.
> Worry is unproductive.
>> Worry is unreasonable.

Worry is Ungodly

The devil has done a number on us. He dangles money and the things money can buy in front of us and has us licking our chops with desire.

Forbes magazine's latest ranking of the world's richest people has Bill Gates perched at the top of the United States' wealthiest for the sixteenth year in a row, with a net worth north of $50 billion.

But Gates' mind-boggling fortune is just a fraction of what Satan offered Jesus. He showed him all the kingdoms of the world and said, *"… if you worship me, it will all be yours" (Luke 4:5-8).*

The bookends of Jesus' life were a borrowed manger and a borrowed tomb. He didn't have a donkey of his own for transportation, didn't own a home, didn't even have a place to lay his head.

"I can change that for you," Satan said. "Worship me and own the world!"

It didn't work on Jesus, but Satan had a hunch that it would on us. And sure enough, he hasn't met much resistance in enticing us to worship money.

In fact he has conned us into using it as our standard of judgment. "What's he worth?" we ask. You know exactly what is meant by the question. We measure a person's worth by his possessions: the size of his house, his car, his job; the size of his paycheck, his bank account, his stock portfolio.

Even at church we kowtow to cash, coddling those with fat wallets. James jabs with a sharp needle:

> *How can you claim that you belong to the Lord Jesus Christ, the Lord of glory, if you show favoritism to rich people and look down on poor people?*
>
> *If a man comes into your church dressed in expensive clothes … and at the same moment another man comes in who is poor and dressed in threadbare clothes, and you make a lot of fuss over the rich man … —well, judging a man by his wealth shows that you are guided by wrong motives.*
>
> *… you are breaking this law of our Lord's when you favor the rich and fawn over them; it is sin (James 2:1-4, 9 TLB).*

In our culture status is based on money: you climb the ladder by earning and accumulating a lot of it. Your self-image is linked to your bank account. You think the devil doesn't get a kick out of that?!

Electronic commercials and print ads are designed to whet our appetite. I count 266 ads in the latest issue of a magazine I subscribe to.

Thirty-one of them plug residential property and furnishings.

Ten promote vehicles.

Forty-four ballyhoo a variety of things: vacation packages, entertainment, conventions, hotels, banks, etc.

And a whopping 181 pitch food, drink, clothes, jewelry, cosmetics, hair care, fragrances, and plastic surgery.

That sounds suspiciously like Jesus' reference to our concern for what we eat, drink, and wear.

When life is saturated with so many wants it's no wonder that there is so much anxiety. When we can't afford what others can our misery meter pegs out.

Jesus was clear: *"You cannot serve both God and Money."* He did not say you *ought not* to serve both, he said you *cannot*.

It's not that work and provision for the future are wrong. The plain teaching of the Bible is that if a man won't work, he shouldn't eat (2 Thessalonians 3:10). Slothfulness and laziness are condemned, and hard work is praised—especially in Proverbs. Work honors God. Planning for the future honors God. It's worry that dishonors God. It is not work and foresight that are forbidden—it is worry.

God and Satan are locked in battle for your trust. God says he will take care of you; Satan says it ain't so. God wants you to trust him; Satan says don't fall for it.

"Surely," wrote William Barclay, "there is no better description of a man's god, than to say that his god is the power in whom he trusts; and when a man puts his trust in material things, then material things have become, not his support, but his god."[1]

> *... do not worry, saying, 'What shall we eat?' or 'What shall we drink?' or 'What shall we wear?' For the pagans run after all these things.*

Could anything please Satan more than seducing Christians to think and act like pagans? He smirks when Christians talk the talk, but don't walk the walk—Christian in name, but pagan in practice.

What does all of this have to do with worry? Just this. Worry is the byproduct of a deceptive idolatry. We wouldn't fall for such obvious idolatry as worshipping Aaron's golden calf, or Nebuchadnezzar's golden statue. But we are easy prey for the idolatry of consumer consumption.

There are two fatal mistakes you can make regarding money. One is to worship it. The other is to worry about it. If Satan can't pull you down with an obsession for accumulating it, he will just as happily push you overboard with anxiety about it. He views the worshipper and the worrier with equal delight. It doesn't matter to him which path you take as long as he succeeds in his ultimate objective—keeping you focused on money rather than on God.

Don't let Satan win this one!

Worry is Unproductive

Jesus makes two points here.

First: *"Who of you by worrying can add a single hour to his life?"*

In other words, what does worry accomplish?

Answer: absolutely nothing!

Well, that's not quite right—there are a few things that worry does for you:

It wrecks your resistance and triggers scads of health problems.

It robs you of optimism and torpedoes your zest for life.

It impairs your judgment, sabotaging your ability to make good decisions.

It makes you unpleasant and unwanted company.

It smothers gratitude; when you worry you are oblivious to blessings.

Those are all *bad* things. Can you name one *good* thing that worry does for you? The only thing I can think of is that it makes you look serious. Hey, hemorrhoids can do that!

Here is Jesus' second point: *"Do not worry about tomorrow … Each day has enough trouble of its own."*

Worry has an active imagination; it sees all sorts of possible problems, most of which never happen. It doubles your trouble: if what you worry about doesn't happen you have lived through it once for nothing; if what you worry about does happen you have lived through it twice.

You will probably live longer, and definitely live happier, by telling those borrowed-from-tomorrow worries to take a hike.

Worry is Unreasonable

There are only two things you can worry about: the things you control, and the things you don't.

It is unreasonable to worry about the things you control because if you control them you can change them.

And it is unreasonable to worry about the things you don't control because if you don't control them there's nothing you can do to change them.

Then there's this: it is unreasonable to worry about things that don't last, like money. You worry that you don't have it. Or not enough of it. Or if you have it you worry that you'll lose it.

Well, that's exactly what's going to happen—you're going to lose it.

> *For we brought nothing into the world, and we can take nothing out of it (1 Timothy 6:7).*

You and Bill Gates are going to check out with exactly the same amount.

In Act III of Thornton Wilder's *Our Town* the narrator takes us on a stroll through the cemetery in Grover's Corners …

We all know that *something* is eternal. And it ain't houses and it ain't names, and it ain't earth, and it ain't even the stars … everybody knows in their bones that *something* is eternal, and that something has to do with human beings. … There's something way down deep that's eternal about every human being. …

You know as well as I do that the dead don't stay interested in us living people for very long. Gradually, gradually, they lose hold of the earth … and the ambitions they had … and the pleasures they had … and the things they suffered …

They get weaned away from earth … they slowly get indifferent to what's goin' on in Grover's Corners … all those terribly important things kind of grow pale around here.[2]

23

YOU DON'T HAVE TO SHOUT

She walked slowly. Head down. Eyes focused an inch in front of her shoes. Always alone. Always.

I saw her nearly every morning just a few blocks from the church where I ministered. The books she carried told me she was a student at the university. I never paid much attention to her. Never wondered who she was, or how her day was going. Or why she was alone.

Until ... that morning.

That morning she wasn't walking, she was sitting on the curb crying. I wondered what was troubling her. Wondered if her feelings had been hurt or her heart had been broken. I thought about stopping to see if I could help, but didn't. I was facing a busy day, an over-crowded schedule. So I drove on to the church, turned the key in my office door, checked my messages, and buckled down to work.

But the image of that crying coed kept muscling its way into my mind, and I decided to go back and talk to her.

I drove to where I'd seen her. She wasn't there. I cruised the area, looking up and down the streets and alleys. I got out of my car and looked through the windows of area shops.

She was gone.

And I never saw her again.

Jesus would have handled that situation very differently. I know, because he did.

> As Jesus approached Jericho, a blind man was sitting by the roadside begging. When he heard the crowd going by, he asked what was happening. They told him, "Jesus of Nazareth is passing by."

He called out, "Jesus, Son of David, have mercy on me!"
Those who led the way rebuked him and told him to be
quiet, but he shouted all the more, "Son of David, have
mercy on me!"

Jesus stopped and ordered the man to be brought to him.
When he came near, Jesus asked him, "What do you want me
to do for you?"

"Lord, I want to see," he replied.

Jesus said to him, "Receive your sight; your faith has healed
you" (Luke 18:35-42).

Do you know what impresses me most in this story?

It's not the persistence of the blind beggar, though that's touching.

It's not the rude rebuke of the disciples telling the beggar to *"shut up"* (MSG), though that's disappointing.

It's not even the healing, though that's thrilling.

What impresses me most are these two words—*Jesus stopped*. *"Jesus stopped and ordered the man to be brought to him" (emphasis mine).*

That's what touches me most. Why? Because by any human measurement Jesus had more pressing concerns at the moment. You see, just before this roadside encounter with the blind beggar Jesus had said to his disciples:

We are going up to Jerusalem, and everything that is written
by the prophets about the Son of Man will be fulfilled. He
will be handed over to the Gentiles. They will mock him,
insult him, spit on him, flog him and kill him (Luke 18:31-
33).

Jesus was on his way to Jerusalem. It would be his last trip. He knew that.

Within hours he would be arrested. He knew that.

He would be tried, convicted, and crucified. He knew that.

Yet, when he heard a plea for help, *Jesus stopped!*

He wasn't sauntering to a leisurely lunch with a friend, mind you. He was racing toward the final hours of his life—staring into the cold eyes of betrayal, torture, and execution. How could he think of anything else? If ever there was a time when he could understandably distance himself from someone else's problem it was now. Instead, he stopped. And helped.

That's what I should have done, and wish I had. I wish I had stopped and sat beside that weeping girl. I don't know what caused her tears, but I wish I hadn't been so busy doing "church work" that I didn't have time to help one of God's hurting children. I wish I hadn't left her sitting on the curb, crying alone.

Know what? I don't remember a single one of those important things that cluttered my calendar that day. But I vividly remember that girl sitting on the curb crying. I still think about her now and then. I wonder where she is—or *if* she is—and if anyone cares. I wonder if anyone ever asked her to dinner, or sent her flowers, or held her hand, or hugged her. I have a feeling that she was starved for companionship.

You may be too. Maybe you've been pushed away by a parent, a child, a spouse. Loneliness is your roommate. You feel the stab of the psalmist's sorrow: *"no one is concerned for me ... no one cares" (Psalm 142:4).*

It Hurts to be Ignored

In a rare chat with his too-busy-to-mess-with-you father, a young boy (I'll call him Tommy) asked, "Daddy, how much do you make an hour?"

"About $300. Why?"

"Just wondered."

Months later Tommy tiptoed into his father's study and stood quietly until he was noticed. Irritated by the interruption dad snapped, "What do you want, Tommy?"

"Daddy ... can I buy an hour of your time?'

"What?!"

Pushing an envelope across the big mahogany desk Tommy said, "I've been saving my money. Here's $300. Can I buy an hour of your time? Just you and me?"

It Hurts to be Neglected

Kids aren't the only ones wounded by neglect. Many elderly parents spend their twilight years in aching aloneness, deserted by their adult children. Weeks, months, years slip by. Letters? Seldom. Phone calls? Few. Visits? Almost never.

I think the psalmist felt the bite of something like that: *"...in my old age, don't set me aside. Don't forsake me now when my strength is failing" (Psalm 71:9 TLB).*

It Hurts to be Rejected

Here on my desk is a letter from a lonely lady:

> *All I want is to be loved. We have all the trappings of success—a 7,500 square foot house, a four-car garage housing three late models and a classic antique, furnishings fit for a palace, and closets crammed with enough stuff to stock a store. But I rarely see my husband. He has no time for me. I don't think he would miss me if I was dead. Sometimes I wish I was.*

Love Without Measure

You know what concerns me? I'm afraid that weeping student not only felt unloved—but unlovable. And I'm afraid that you may be feeling the same way. How could God love someone like me? you wonder.

Measured by harsh human judgment, Jesus' list-of-the-loved includes some unlikely characters:

> An adulteress in Jerusalem (John 8:1-11).
> A five-times-divorced woman in Samaria (John 4:7-30).
> A lowlife tax collector in Jericho (Luke 19:1-9).

The true measure of God's love is that he loves without measure: his love is *"too wonderful to be measured" (Ephesians 3:19 CEV)*. Don't try to measure the immeasurable—He loves you more than you can imagine. And he thinks about you constantly.

I just did the math, and find that I had been bunking on God's good earth for 25,996 days when my 99-year-old mother died. It would be a safe bet that she thought about me for at least a few minutes every one of those 25,996 days.

But God thinks about me even more: he thinks about me all the time; every minute of every day.

You too. He is always thinking about you.

He is thinking about me right now as I write this sentence. And he is thinking about you right now—weeks, months, or years later—as you read it.

Was that roadside beggar worthy of Jesus' attention? What sins lurked in the shadows of his past? And what about his future? If Jesus restored his sight how would he use it? To look with gratitude or to look with lust?

Jesus knew that some of those he healed would misuse the blessing; knew that some he made healthy would not be holy. Every time he blessed he had to overlook the past—and the future.

Aren't you glad that he still does? He doesn't ask you to prove in advance that if he blesses you financially you will be a faithful steward. He doesn't shut off your oxygen supply when you misuse his gifts. He doesn't take away the gifts he's given because you forget to say "thank you."

However flawed your *past*, and however you choose to use your *future*, Jesus is sympathetic to your *present* problems. When he hears your cry for help, Jesus stops!

The reason I find that so impressive is because in my little world the most important things that happen each day are the things that happen to *me*!

A doctor's appointment.
Reading the mail.
Getting the oil changed.
Deciding where to have lunch.

Preoccupied with such pressing matters, it's difficult for me to stop what I'm doing long enough to be interested in what you're doing.

The blind man shouted to get Jesus' attention. And Jesus stopped.

That crying coed didn't shout. And I didn't stop.

And you don't have to shout, because he is *"watching everything that concerns you!"*

> *Let him have all your worries and cares,*
> *for he is always thinking about you and*
> *watching everything that concerns you.*

24

I CHOOSE PEACE

M isty Ann Weaver is in prison. She'll be bunking there for the next twenty-five years. Misty is not a bad person, but she made a bad mistake. She started a fire that killed some people.

Why did she do it? Well, bizarre as it sounds, Misty *set* the fire to keep from *getting* fired. You see, she was responsible for pulling together the paperwork for a recertification audit for her boss. She couldn't get it done by the deadline and she was afraid she would be fired for it. She was up to her chin in financial problems, and couldn't risk losing her job. She thought a small wastebasket fire would delay the audit, but that small fire turned into a roaring four-alarm inferno. Three dead. Another six injured.

The evening news on the day of her arrest showed footage of Misty in handcuffs, with a towel over her head. On the same newscast a Hollywood star who had just won a coveted award was interviewed. Noting that he clocked in at $20 million per film, and was now adding this prize to his crowded trophy case the interviewer asked, "What's left? You seem to have everything. Is there anything that you still want?" With a faraway look in his eyes the actor said, "Yes, one thing—peace."

Misty didn't have anything. The Hollywood star had everything. Neither had peace.

Peace is more a matter of mind than of circumstances. Your financial picture may be dismal, your schedule demanding, and your health dicey, yet you may be doing quite well. On the other hand, you may have a fat bank balance, a leisurely life, and tip-top health, yet find peace a distant dream. "The most miserable people I have known," said Sydney Harris, "have not been those who suffered from catastrophes—which they could blame on fate or accident—but those who had everything they wanted, except the power to enjoy it."

Without peace of mind nothing you accomplish will mean much. But with peace of mind nothing can derail your sense of contentment and joy.

How do you achieve it? I have a few suggestions.

Stop Looking in the Wrong Places

The search for peace of mind often turns to the gods of this world rather than to the God who *made* this world.

> We worship the god of money, only to learn that there are things that money cannot buy, and that in a seesaw economy it is a fickle and unreliable deity.

> We bow before the god of pleasure, only to discover that its thrills play out and its passions are short-lived.

> We kneel before the god of science, only to find that while it has given us many good things, it has also fathered fears that it can't calm.

It is short-sighted to depend on short-term gods. They don't deliver on their promises. Only the eternal God does that: *"You, Lord, give true peace to those who depend on you"* (Isaiah 26:3 NCV).

Be an Instrument of Peace

The prayer of Francis of Assisi, beautiful in its simplicity, is one of history's most moving prayers:

Lord,
Make me an instrument of thy peace.
Where there is hatred, let me sow love;
Where there is injury, pardon;
Where there is doubt, faith;
Where there is despair, hope;
Where there is darkness, light;
Where there is sadness, joy.

O divine Master,
Grant that I may not so much seek
To be consoled as to console,
To be understood as to understand,
To be loved as to love;
For it is in giving that we receive;
It is in pardoning that we are pardoned;
It is in dying to self that we are born to eternal life.

Most prayers are self-centered. But this one is others-centered, asking to be used as an envoy of peace in a world of turbulence: an emissary of love where there is hatred, faith where there is doubt, hope where there is despair, light where there is darkness, joy where there is sadness. It breaks free of pettiness, faultfinding, and combativeness, bringing with it the serendipitous gift of personal peace.

Early on we develop a sense of entitlement, and many never grow out of it. We demand that others console *us*, understand *us*, love *us*, and give to *us*. But in this prayer we ask to be the one who consoles *others*, understands *others*, loves *others*, and gives to *others*.

And it brings peace, for in becoming an instrument of peace, you also become a recipient of peace.

Let the Peace of Christ Rule

Later in the evening Jesus will be betrayed, arrested and tried. But now he is in the upper room with his disciples to eat the Passover meal.

He breaks the bread: *"This is my body."*
He gives them the cup: *"This is my blood."*

They reel in dazed disbelief when he tells them, *"one of you is going to betray me."* Then the knockout blow: *"I will be with you only a little longer"* (John 13:21, 33).

In light of those woeful words what he says minutes later has the smell of absurdity: *"Peace I leave with you; my peace I give you ... Do not let your hearts be troubled and do not be afraid"* (John 14:27).

The next two days fall far short of that promised peace—two days packed with one disaster after another: betrayal, arrest, trials, crucifixion. Their world is in chaos, their hopes shattered. *"Peace I give you,"* he said. Well, so much for that! He is dead, and they are on the run!

On Sunday evening they back-alley their way to the upper room again. Terrified that what has happened to him will now happen to them, they lock the door and ponder their next move.

Suddenly Jesus appears! And speaks! "Greetings, cowards!"

No! That's what I would have said, but that's not what he says. He says, *"Peace be with you!"* (John 20:19). What an unthinkable thing to say to those who had deserted him when he needed them most. The last time he had seen them he had seen only their backs, as they ran for their lives, leaving him to face a blood-thirsty mob alone. And the last words he had heard come from Peter's mouth were, *"I don't know this man."*

So the first words he speaks to them now are the last words they expect to hear: *"Peace be with you!"*

The words seem as far-fetched now as they did before, for the atmosphere in this room is anything but peaceful: they are frightened and confused—and now forced to face the one they had abandoned. The air is electric with danger—and shame. But he makes no mention of their

168

desertion. He simply validates his identity by showing them the crucifixion wounds—his hands and his side—then says it again, *"Peace be with you" (John 20: 21).*

One of the disciples—Thomas—wasn't there that night. When they told him they had seen Jesus, he scoffed: *"Unless I see the nail marks in his hands and put my finger where the nails were, and put my hand into his side, I will not believe it."*

A week later they come to this room again—Thomas too. And again they lock the door.

And again Jesus appears.

His message? Yes, the same—*"Peace be with you" (John 20: 26).*

The words are still hard to swallow. The crucifixion is past, but the danger isn't. Persecution and violence lurk outside that door. The mood in this room is painted in the dull grays of shattered dreams, disillusionment, grief, and panic. Nothing that evokes a spirit of peace.

Yet, that is what Jesus promises. When they first met in this room Jesus said, *"Peace I leave with you; my peace I give you."* And the next two times he sees them—even in the face of their past failures and their future trials—he sings the same chorus:

> *peace be with you;*
> *peace be with you.*

Exercise Your Right to Choose

Your life is noisy, right?

First thing in the morning the alarm clock catapults you from peace to panic. The children get up grumpy. Your spouse doesn't make the cut for today's *Sing-and-be-Happy* list. You bring in the paper—along with a wad of gum on your shoe. You slump into your chair at the kitchen table, and sit in cat barf. You spill the milk. You're late for work. Your boss doesn't make the *Sing-and-be-Happy* list either. Everyone's problem lands in your lap. *Plop! Thud!* One hassle after another has your name on it.

At the end of the day you're drained. You would like nothing better than to kick back in your favorite chair for an hour. Not a chance. There are kids to pick up, dinner to prepare, dishes to wash, beds to change, clothes to launder ... a school conference, a committee meeting, a report to prepare.

The first sentence of Max Ehrmann's *Desiderata* advises: *"Go placidly amid the noise and haste, and remember what peace there may be in silence."* Oh, if only!

Or is yours the opposite problem? Single? Widowed? Your life is far too quiet. You would welcome a little noise, would love for the phone to ring.

Certain people are able push your buttons and drive you to within a couple of degrees of certifiable insanity. An out-of-control child. An always-on-your-case parent. A you-can't-do-anything-right spouse. A know-it-all associate. A cantankerous church member.

Thoughts that splinter your peace go something like this:

> If only my spouse was more understanding I wouldn't be so stressed.

> If only my child was more respectful I wouldn't be so upset.

> If only my boss was more considerate ...

> If only I didn't have to deal with this impossibly-difficult person ...

> If only I wasn't buried under these financial problems ...

> If only the weather was dryer—or wetter; hotter—or cooler ...

> If only my world was the way I think it should be I would be happy and at peace.

No you wouldn't. Peace of mind is not circumstance driven. It's an inside job. It is not events that determine your level of peace, it is how you react to those events. You don't have to cede control of your life to people or circumstances.

Here are two sentences that can keep you in control: *I have the right to choose. I choose peace.*

> When some motor-mouth poisons the water, say to yourself: I have the right to choose. I can choose to be upset or I can choose peace. I choose peace.

> When you are hammered by unfair demands, say to yourself: I have the right to choose. I can choose to let this get to me or I can choose peace. I choose peace.

> When some Andretti-wannabe cuts you off and you're bordering on road rage, say to yourself: I have the right to choose. I can choose to give this turkey control of my blood pressure or I can choose peace. I choose peace.

> When the TV goes on the fritz, say to yourself: I have the right to choose. I can choose to let this ruin my day or I can choose peace. I choose peace.

> When the computer blinks and goes black and your last three hours of work disappear forever into the cyberspace cemetery, say to yourself: I have the right to choose. I can choose to fly off the handle and do some real damage here or I can choose peace. I choose peace.

Well, there they are—two sentences that pry control of your life out of the hands of people and circumstances and put you in the driver's seat: *I have the right to choose. I choose peace.*

Two sentences that make it impossible for anyone or anything to hijack your peace without your consent: *I have the right to choose. I choose peace.*

Two sentences that convert your noisy world into a peaceful one: *I have the right to choose. I choose peace.*

> *Let him have all your worries and cares,*
> *for he is always thinking about you and*
> *watching everything that concerns you.*

25

I KNOW HE WATCHES ME

On Tuesday, September 11, 2001, I punched off the alarm, tossed back the covers, crawled out of bed, pulled on my sweats, laced up my Asics, and stepped out the door for my morning jog.

Back inside an hour later I showered, shaved, dressed, and headed to my office.

I stopped at the 7-Eleven at 34th and Frankford, poured a cup o' joe, pulled a newspaper from the rack, and moseyed up to the checkout counter.

"Can you believe it?" sputtered the cashier.

"Believe what?" I asked, more interested in my paper than in her answer.

"The World Trade Center thing!"

"What World Trade Center thing?"

"Haven't you heard? Two planes crashed into the World Trade Center towers!"

Driving the remaining six blocks to my office I kept thinking, "She has to be mistaken!" At my desk I booted my computer and logged onto CNN. As you know, she wasn't mistaken.

The number of injured, dead, and buried alive was numbing. I was still scrolling through the news when the phone rang.

"Mr. Barnett?"

"Yes."

"Dr. Avant wants to speak to you. Can you hold, please?"

Uh-oh! My blood draws the past few months had signaled rising PSA levels. Dr. Avant, my friend and physician, had ordered a biopsy the previous week.

"Joe?"

"Hi doc." (I sounded like I'd been sucking helium.)

"Joe, the biopsy was positive."

Cancer!

I had *cancer.*

Can-cer! Two syllables that grip your gut and buckle your knees. Bravado took a hike. My mortality hadn't crossed my mind in a long time. It did now!

"Dear God …"

Did he know?

Did he care?

At that moment he had his hands full with thousands of casualties in New York. How could he be concerned about me, one victim of prostate cancer in Texas?

The answer is theologized in cold, grandiose words like omniscient, omnipotent, and omnipresent—meaning that God is aware enough and powerful enough and everywhere enough to listen to the prayers and care for the concerns of his children in New York and Texas—and everywhere else—at the same time.

Yes, he knew.

Yes, he cared.

That's what my head said. That's what my sermons said. But that's not what my 100-beats-per-minute heart-rate said.

Measured by the catastrophe in New York, my problem was minor. I knew that. But it didn't eliminate my anxiety. Neither did the internet article that I googled that told me 220,000 men would be diagnosed with prostate cancer in the next 12 months. Knowing where I stood as a statistic didn't help much.[1]

Can you identify with that? Anything eating at you, sending your blood-pressure through the roof?

Health gone bad?

Marriage gone sour?

Child gone haywire?
Finances gone south?
Hopes gone belly up?

What I needed on 9/11 was God. And maybe God is what you're needing right now. Listen, whatever is bothering you isn't a minor matter. If others think so, they're mistaken! If it concerns you, it concerns him. He is *"watching everything that concerns you."*

Mind-boggling isn't it? To think that he is concerned about your concerns when he has so many other things to be concerned about? Things like ...

Eight hundred million people going to bed hungry every night.

Terrorists flying airplanes into skyscrapers.

Suicide bombers strapping explosives to their chests and blowing people to bits on crowded streets.

The never-ending Israeli-Palestinian mess.

All this, and he is concerned about you? Absolutely!

You Have His Attention

Three months before the Presidential election I received an engraved invitation from a committee made up of members of the United States Congress, inviting me to attend The President's Dinner.

Impressed? No? Well, you will be when I tell you that enclosed with my invitation was a letter from the President himself, telling me how honored he and the First Lady would be to have me attend.

The caveat? They wanted me to pony up $2,500 to hobnob with the high-ups. I thought about it, but decided against it, because there would have been so many egos elbowing for the President's attention that he wouldn't have been able to spend as much time with me as he'd want to. So I decided to wait until things settled down, after the election. Then I'd hop a plane, drop my duds in the Lincoln bedroom and hang out for a couple of days at the White House with the President and First Lady; spend some quality time together, you know? (Why are you grinning?)

Can you get the President's attention? Probably not.

Can you get God's attention? You already have.

When David scanned the sky, he stroked his beard, shook his head and mused:

> *When I look at the night sky and see the work of your fingers—the moon and the stars you have set in place—what are mortals that you should think of us, mere humans that you should care for us? (Psalm 8:3-4 NLT).*

Stargazing can do that to you—make you feel small and insignificant. But don't fool yourself, there's not a star in the sky that has a smidgen of your value. God is crazy about you. He is always thinking about you!

Earthly relationships are fragile. Heavenly ones aren't.

Your parent may ignore you.
Your child may neglect you.
Your spouse may abandon you.
But your Father won't forget you.

> *Not even a sparrow, worth only half a penny, can fall to the ground without your Father knowing it. ...So don't be afraid; you are more valuable to him than a whole flock of sparrows (Matthew 10:29, 31 NLT).*

For a musician, Starbucks on 51st and Broadway in Manhattan is one of the most lucrative locations in the world. Tips can be substantial if an entertainer connects with the *caffe latte* crowd. John Oaks was connecting. During his rendition of *If You Don't Know Me by Now* John noticed a lady swaying to the beat and singing along.

After the tune was over she approached him. "I apologize for singing along on that song. Did it bother you?" she asked.

"No," he said. "I love it when the audience joins in. Would you like to sing up front on the next selection?"

To his surprise she said yes.

"What are you in the mood to sing?"

"Well ... do you know any hymns?"

Did he ever! He'd cut his teeth on hymns. "How about *His Eye is on the Sparrow?*"

She was silent, her eyes averted. Then she locked eyes with him and said, "Yeah, let's do *that* one."

She put down her purse, straightened her jacket and faced the center of the shop. John did a two-bar setup, and she began to sing.

> *Why should I be discouraged?*
> *Why should the shadows come?*

The audience of coffee drinkers was transfixed. Even the gurgling of the cappuccino machine ceased as the employees stopped what they were doing to listen. The song rose to its conclusion.

> *I sing because I'm happy;*
> *I sing because I'm free.*
> *For His eye is on the sparrow*
> *And I know He watches me.*

When the last note was sung the applause crescendoed to a roar that would have done Carnegie Hall proud. John embraced his new friend. "That was beautiful!" he said.

"It's funny that you picked that hymn," she said.

"Why is that?"

"Well..." she hesitated, "that was my daughter's favorite song." She took his hands. "She was 16. She died of a brain tumor last week."

John was stunned, and silent. Finally, he stammered, "Are you going to be okay?"

She smiled through tear-filled eyes and squeezed his hands. "I'm gonna be okay. I've just got to keep trusting the Lord and singing his songs, and everything's gonna be just fine."[2]

I sing because I'm happy;
I sing because I'm free.
For His eye is on the sparrow
And I know He watches me.

Let him have all your worries and cares,
for he is always thinking about you and
watching everything that concerns you.

Summary Resolutions from Section Five

PEACE

Let him have all your worries and cares,
for he is always thinking about you and
watching everything that concerns you.
—1 Peter 5:7 TLB

I RESOLVE to be an agent of love where there is hatred, faith where there is doubt, hope where there is despair, light where there is darkness, joy where there is sadness.

I RESOLVE not to worry about *anything*, to pray about *everything*, and to think about the *right things*.

I RESOLVE to remember that nothing that troubles me is too small for God's concern, and nothing too large for him to handle.

I RESOLVE to remember that it is not circumstances that determine my level of peace, but how I react to circumstances.

I RESOLVE to maintain control of my mood by exercising my right to choose—I choose peace.

I RESOLVE to remember that God's eye is on the sparrow, and he always watches me.

SECTION SIX

JOY

This is the day the Lord has made;
let us rejoice and be glad in it.
—PSALM 118:24

❧

Rejoice in the Lord always. I will say it again: Rejoice!
(Philippians 4:4).

❧

Have your dreams been derailed? Does life seem to be an endless string of bills and pills? Has grief has come calling? Do your prayers seem to go unheard and unanswered? If so, you may be tempted to skip this section. The last thing you need is for someone to try to force-feed you a joy pill: *"C'mon, be happy! Lots of people have bigger problems than you!"* That kind of comment makes you want to hurt somebody.

You've learned the hard way that you're not going to get through life without storms—in your family, in the workplace, probably in your church.

So when Paul says, *"Be joyful always!" (1 Thessalonians 5:16)* your response may be, "Get real! You can't hide from a hurricane under a beach umbrella!"

And he isn't finished: *"... we also rejoice in our sufferings ... (Romans 5:3).* What?!

He doesn't deny our sufferings. Neither does he define them. Why? Probably because your suffering is different from mine, and mine from yours, and ours from others. Your suffering is uniquely yours; it has your name on it.

Your Bible is straight up on this: it warns that life won't be all sunshine and summertime. There will be dark, cold, stormy days.

But it also stakes your claim to joy. Not counterfeit joy. The real thing!

So stay with me for this final section.

26

TODAY'S TREASURES, TOMORROW'S RUINS

Barry Schwartz went to the GAP to buy a new pair of jeans. The salesperson asked, "Do you want them slim fit, easy fit, relaxed fit, baggy, or extra baggy? Do you want them stonewashed, acid-washed, or distressed? Do you want them button-fly or zipper-fly? Do you want them faded or regular?"

Barry sputtered, "I just want regular jeans. You know, the kind that used to be the only kind."[1]

A few days later, scanning the shelves of his local supermarket, Barry counted 85 brands of crackers, 285 varieties of cookies, 230 soups, 275 cereals, 175 salad dressings, and 64 barbecue sauces.

He found 80 pain relievers, 90 cold remedies and decongestants, 61 varieties of suntan oil, 116 kinds of skin cream, 360 shampoos, 40 toothpastes, 150 lipsticks, 75 eyeliners, and 90 colors of nail polish.[2]

There was a time when product choices were few. Now they seem limitless. Savvy marketers keep our desires a fingertip beyond our reach, wanting to make sure that our wants outrun our ability to satisfy them.

This profusion of choices sloshes over into big ticket items. We are duped into believing that happiness is found in a new home, a new car, a new wardrobe. But it doesn't take long for the new to wear off, and then the itch to trade up needs to be scratched again.

It even intrudes on relationships. Husbands dump wives because they think someone else will make them happy. Wives ditch husbands because they think someone else will provide the excitement they're missing.

These insatiable wants need to be put in perspective. One way to do that is to see how short-lived this world's treasures are.

Future Ruins

Babylon was once the largest city in the world. Its *Hanging Gardens*, with its astounding irrigation system, was one of the *Seven Wonders of the World*. Nebuchadnezzar's palace was a jaw-dropping monument to opulence. But Babylon is no more. Only a memory. A ruin.

Ephesus, at one time the capital of Proconsular Asia, was also the home of one of the *Seven Wonders of the World*: the *Temple of Artemis*— the largest building of the ancient world. Ephesus turned heads with its Library of Celsus, its 25,000-seat open-air theatre, and the most advanced aqueduct system in the world. But this magnificent city, which had a population of 500,000 in 100 A.D., has been gone since the 15ᵗʰ century. Only a memory. A ruin.

The 21ˢᵗ century displays a plethora of eye-popping prosperity ...

> ... stunning skyscrapers, elegant high-rises, and palatial mansions in suburbia's gated enclaves;
> ... multi-layered, multi-laned freeways;
> ... trendy upscale shops, classy hotels, and high-dollar restaurants.

Closer to home, put this book in your lap and survey your where-you-are-right-now surroundings. Pretty nice, huh?

You might even want to have a look at your church. Not bad.

Future ruins!

All of them!

The time will come when these dazzling buildings, stylish shops, and lavish surroundings will be nothing but rubble, gawked at by tourists. Today's treasures are tomorrow's ruins. Don't put too much stock in them.

Solomon can tell you that pleasure, power, and possessions don't live up to their promises. He had it all: *"I denied myself nothing my eyes desired,"* he said. *"I refused my heart no pleasure" (Ecclesiastes 2:10).* If he wanted it, he got it. Nothing was out of reach: nothing too expensive, nothing too extravagant. A romp through Ecclesiastes will leave you wide-eyed and breathless.

> *I undertook great projects: I built houses for myself and planted vineyards. I made gardens and parks and planted all kinds of fruit trees in them. I made reservoirs to water groves of flourishing trees. I bought male and female slaves and had other slaves who were born in my house. I also owned more herds and flocks than anyone in Jerusalem before me. I amassed silver and gold for myself ... I acquired men and women singers, and a harem as well ... I became greater by far than anyone in Jerusalem before me (Ecclesiastes 2:4-9).*

The queen of Sheba, certainly no stranger to luxury, came to check Solomon out. She didn't come empty-handed either. She brought a boatload of loot: four and a half tons of gold, and a shipload of spices and precious gems. How's that for a host gift? But Solomon one-upped her when she headed home by loading her boat with more than she had brought. His lifestyle took her breath away.[3]

But what left her—and us—breathless, left him bitter ...

> *"Utterly meaningless!"* he said (Ecclesiastes 1:2).
> *"Like chasing the wind,"* he said (Ecclesiastes 1:14 NLT).
> *"I hated life,"* he said (Ecclesiastes 2:17).

It's Not What You Have—But Who You Are that Counts

French-Canadian broadcaster Robert Blondin interviewed more than 600 people in countries as diverse as Sweden, China, and the United States.

He asked just one question: "What makes people happy?" The answers were pretty much the same everywhere ...

> People are happy because they are in control of their attitudes.

People are happy because they are absorbed in their families, their friends, their work, and causes they believe in.

People are happy because they are a part of something bigger than themselves.

People are happy because of inner values, not because of outer circumstances.

People are happy because of who they are, not because of what they have.

The conclusion was clear: happiness comes from inner stability, not from outer security. No matter how much money they make, how plush the house they live in, how well known they are, or how much power they have, people are happy only if they have *inner* peace.

Blondin's findings fly in the face of our belief that certain conditions promise joy, and the absence of those conditions promise misery; belief that happiness depends on wealth, health, or marriage—even though we see scads of wealthy, healthy, married people who are miserable; belief that inner happiness depends on outer circumstances.

Outer circumstances are temporary. Whether you're a dishwasher or head honcho, it's a temporary job. Whether you live in a shack or a mansion, it's temporary housing. If your happiness is tied to the temporary you are terribly vulnerable.

One sure way to miss joy is to hitch your happiness to things that can't produce it, things that in the long run are meaningless, things that are temporary.

So we fix our eyes not on what is seen, but on what is unseen. For what is seen is temporary, but what is unseen is eternal (2 Corinthians 4:18).

Focus on the meaningful and permanent—and enjoy this day.

> *This is the day the Lord has made;*
> *let us rejoice and be glad in it.*

27

YOU'RE THE ONLY
YOU IN THE WORLD

The name may not ring a bell, but I'm pretty sure you know Paul Orfalea. Let me tell you about him and see if it comes to you.

Paul couldn't read. He faked his way through first and second grades. Almost. Near the end of the second grade his teacher caught on to him and flunked him.

Paul got use to failure. People thought he was dumb as a turnip. He even did a stretch in a school for retarded children. The fact is he was dyslexic, but it was a long time before someone finally put their finger on the problem. He eventually graduated from high school—1492nd in a class of 1500.

Paul has this advice for you: *"Work with your strengths, not your weaknesses. If you're not good at something, do something else. Go where you are strong."*

That's what Paul did. He borrowed money to open a copy shop in the corner of a hamburger joint—with only one copy machine. The reason I think you know Paul is because I'm pretty sure you've heard of his copy shop. It's the one with the goofy name—*Kinko's*. Paul grew *Kinko's* to more than 1,400 stores in 11 countries, and then sold it to FedEx for $2.4 billion.

Paul followed his own advice: *"Work with your strengths, not your weaknesses. ... Go where you are strong."*

To find that place—and the joy that's found there—there are a couple of things you have to do.

First, you have to …

Make Peace with Who You Are

Dr. Batsell Baxter was a well-known, highly-respected preacher in Nashville, Tennessee. One Sunday he took a seat on the front pew after delivering his sermon. A cute kid got away from his mother, trotted to the front of the church and squeezed in next to Dr. Baxter. Leaning close to him he whispered, *"I wisht I wuz you!"*

That's not just kid stuff. You've done it I bet; fixed an envious eye on someone who seems to have it all—a movie star, a sports hero, a wealthy businessperson—and thought, *"I wisht I wuz you!"*

Don't go there!

Not that these high-profile heavy-hitters aren't important. They are. But it's not because they mesmerize us with their acting talent. It's not because they thrill us with their ability to run, throw, catch, kick, shoot, jump, or skate. And it's not because they have the Midas touch. They're important because God made them who they are, and because God loves them as they are.

In other words, they are important for the same reason you are: because God made you who you are, and because God loves you as you are.

You are exactly who God wants you to be. If he had wanted you to be a movie star, a sports star, or a business czar he could have pulled it off. If he had wanted you to be a Dr. Baxter, a Martin Luther, an apostle Paul, or a Moses, he could have made it happen. But he made you who he wanted you to be—*you!* There is no one else in the world like you. Never has been. Never will be. You are an original. One-of-a-kind. You're the only *you* in the world. That's who God made you. And he didn't make a mistake.

Poor Paul. Not Paul Orfalea, but Paul the apostle. He apparently didn't have much going for him in the looks department. One account says that he was "baldheaded and bowlegged ... small in size, with meeting eyebrows, and a large, crooked nose." There may be something to that unflattering description, because his critics at Corinth sniped at his appearance—and his preaching:

> *His letters are weighty and forceful, but in person he is unimpressive and his speaking amounts to nothing (2 Corinthians 10:10).*

The Living Bible has that last phrase this way: *"You have never heard a worse preacher."* Ouch!

But I don't need to remind you of his strengths: he started a bevy of churches, and wrote half the books in your New Testament.

"Work with your strengths ... Go where you are strong" advises Paul Orfalea. Paul the apostle would agree. In fact, he said it first:

> *God has given each of us the ability to do certain things well. So if God has given you the ability to prophesy, speak out ... If your gift is that of serving others, serve them well. If you are a teacher, do a good job of teaching. If your gift is to encourage others, do it! If you have money, share it generously. If God has given you leadership ability, take the responsibility seriously. And if you have a gift for showing kindness to others, do it gladly (Romans 12:6-8 NLT).*

As he said to his protégé, Timothy: *"Do not neglect your gift ... "* *(1 Timothy 4:14).*

You don't have everything. But you have something. We'll all be diminished if you don't use it.

When Jesus was about to go to Jerusalem for the last time he told two of his disciples, *"Go to the village ... as you enter it, you will find a colt tied there ... Untie it and bring it here. If anyone asks you, 'Why are you untying it?' tell him, 'The Lord needs it'"* *(Luke 19:30-31).*

Does the Lord really need anything? He did that day. Prophecy had said: *"... your king comes to you ... gentle and riding on a donkey" (Zechariah 9:9).* Jesus didn't own a donkey; he needed to borrow that one.

You, too, have something that the Lord needs—something that none of the rest of us has. He needs it. We all need it. We need *you!*

You have strengths. You are special!

When Leonard Bernstein, the distinguished orchestra conductor, was asked, "What is the most difficult instrument to play?" he answered:

> *Second fiddle. I can get plenty of first violinists, but to find one who plays second violin with as much enthusiasm ... now that's a challenge.*

The apostle Paul knew the value of second fiddles. He wouldn't have survived, and couldn't have served, without them. He did his rookie preaching in Damascus, where a pack of militant firebrands, irritated by his conversion, plotted to assassinate him. They kept an around-the-clock eye on the city gates, determined to drop him in his tracks the minute he left town. But some of the Damascus disciples did an end-run on them. Bypassing the gates, they prowled the city wall, and at an obscure site lowered Paul to the ground in a big basket. And he hit the ground running.

Who were the members of this basket brigade? No one knows. Not one name is recorded. Just a bunch of second fiddles who saved the life of the man who became Christianity's best-known spokesperson. You've never heard their names, but without them you would never have heard Paul's name.

Paul wrote Romans from Corinth, 1500 miles from Rome. Who would step up and deliver his letter? A second fiddle named Phoebe. She could never have written Romans, Christianity's most important theological document. But she made the treacherous 1500-mile trek with it tucked under her robe. In the last chapter of Romans Paul salutes some special people. Phoebe leads the list. There are others—twenty-seven in all—who are mentioned by name. A few you have heard of. Most you haven't. A bunch of second fiddles.

Think you're a second fiddle? That's not a bad thing to be.

So walk away from that *"I wisht I wuz you!"* stuff!

"I wish I was Moses."

"I wish I was Paul."

"I wish I was (fill in the blank)."

God already has a Moses! God already has a Paul! God already has a ...! But you're the only you he has! And he needs you just as much as he needed them.

Being happy is making peace with who you are and with what you can do—and refusing to beat up on yourself for who you aren't and for what you can't do.

The second thing you have to do to be happy is ...

Make Peace with Your Past

That means learning to live with the choices you've made—and with the choices that have been made for you.

There are some choices that impact your life in which you didn't have a voice or a vote. You didn't choose your parents, your gender, your race, or your time in history. These choices were made for you.

On the other hand, many of the choices that have made your life what it is were yours, and only yours. You chose your spouse, your career, your religion, your place of residence. You made those choices without fully knowing their outcome. Some of them are reversible. Some aren't.

Making peace with your past is a Three-Act play.

> *ACT I – Appreciation.* There are some things that you can look back on and appreciate: you had loving parents, were born in a great country, live at a favored time in history, received a good education, and married well.

> *ACT II – Understanding.* There are some things that you can't appreciate, but you can understand why they

195

happened: your parents' divorce, your father's lack of positive support, your mother's alcoholism.

ACT III – Forgiveness. When neither appreciation nor understanding is possible, hopefully you can reach down deep and forgive. Happiness is impossible without forgiveness; bitterness and happiness can't live together.

This Three-Act package permits you to breathe the fresh air of reconciliation—of making peace with all that has brought you to where you are.

When you make peace with your past you open the door to joy—to the exhilaration of knowing that you have the capacity to creatively respond to whatever challenges are thrown at you.

Jeffrey Sonnenfeld and Andrew Ward, in the closing lines of their book *Firing Back* wrote:

> *... we have choices in life even in defeat. ... No one can truly define success and failure for us—only we can define them for ourselves. No one can take away our dignity unless we surrender it. No one can take away our hope and pride unless we give up. No one can take away our love for those others around us who believe in us—unless we elect to ignore them. ... No one can steal our creativity, imagination, and skills unless we stop thinking. No one can take away our humor unless we forget to smile. No one can take away our hope and opportunity for tomorrow unless we close our own eyes.[1]*

Make peace with who you are. Celebrate your individuality. And make peace with your past. Celebrate the present and future. And enjoy this wonderful day.

> *This is the day the Lord has made;*
> *let us rejoice and be glad in it.*

28

YOU CAN MAKE A DIFFERENCE

Alternately twisting a strand of hair and dabbing her eyes with a small handkerchief, Ing told me about watching her father, her mother, her husband, and two of her babies slowly starve to death. She escaped Cambodia with her young son, the only other surviving member of her family.

In Cambodia, before the horrors of war, poverty, and starvation, Ing was a teacher. Here, in the unfamiliar United States, she was cleaning houses during the day and hotel restrooms at night. She and her son lived in a low rent area, festering with crime. A couple of run-ins with drug dealers had left her terrified. She parked several blocks away from home each evening, slunk through back-alley darkness, and squeezed through a window into her apartment.

At the time I met Ing I had two articles on my desk which I had been perusing with a mixture of amusement and sadness. One was a written debate on Bible inerrancy, focusing on the Exodus account of the 430-year Israelite sojourn in Egypt. The disputants were arguing the skipped-generation theory: whether there were two Amrams or only one. The second article was an installment of the hot issue in my religious group at the time—the "New Hermeneutic versus the Old Hermeneutic."

Returning home after listening to Ing's story, I found that I didn't have the stomach for skipped-generations or hermeneutic hysterics. Looking into the hollow eyes of this frail, frightened woman who had cradled her babies in her arms while they died had given me a drastically altered sense of what was important.

You may never meet a person like Ing. Perhaps you live in a place where you rarely, if ever, encounter people in poverty. But wherever you live, you inevitably cross paths with someone who is hurting. Joy comes when you respond to God's nudging, becoming his instrument of blessing to that person—from knowing that you made a difference.

Don't know what to do? Here are a couple of things to get you started.

Pray for Someone

Jim Wood had been ministering at his new church only a few weeks when he got a call from Clyde, one of his parishioners, asking him to go for a drive with him. Clyde was a very quiet guy, and as they cruised through town he didn't say a word. He drove out into the country, parked by the side of the road, opened the trunk, pulled out two aluminum chairs, and walked out into the field. Jim followed. Clyde set the chairs under a large oak tree and the two sat down. He still didn't speak, and Jim found the silence uncomfortable. After awhile he said, "Well, this is a beautiful place, Clyde."

"Yeah," Clyde said. "This is my tree."

"You own this property?"

"No, it belongs to a friend of mine, but he gave me this tree. I come out here and sit, and think, and pray."

More silence. Finally, Clyde said, "Jim, I want to pray for you." And he did. Prayed for his ministry. His family. His health. His happiness. Then he got up, put the chairs back in the car, drove back to the church, and told Jim goodbye.

A few days later Jim was having breakfast with one of the men from his church. "I saw you with Clyde the other day," he said. "Did he drive you out into the country?"

"Yeah," Jim said.

"Did you just sit there for awhile, no one saying anything?"

"Yeah."

"Did he pray for you?"

"Yeah."

"Let me tell you how I met Clyde," he said. "The week before I got married he called me and said he wanted me to go for a drive with him. He took me out to his tree. We sat for a long time without a word being spoken. Then Clyde said he wanted to pray for me. He prayed a wonderful prayer for our marriage, and then brought me back to town."

A young man in the next booth overheard the conversation, and turning to the two men said, "May I tell you how I met Clyde? My wife and I were devastated when our first baby was stillborn. Less than a week after our loss, Clyde called and said he wanted me to take a drive with him. He took me out to his tree. We sat in silence for awhile, and then he said he wanted to pray for me. And he did."[1]

Clyde had been doing that for a long time—his own quiet, powerful ministry.

You don't have to do it Clyde's way. Probably shouldn't. You might be uncomfortable with it, and others almost certainly would be. But you can have a prayer list, and should. Be concerned enough about others to think about them, and to take their names to the throne. You don't have to tell them that you're praying for them, but it's okay if you do. They will find comfort—and you will find joy.

Help Someone

Landing a teaching position at a prestigious university was thrilling for the recent doctoral graduate, mainly because there was a tenured professor there who was her hero. She had read everything he had written, and had dreamed of being mentored by him. She was so anxious to meet him that she went to his office before her books were unpacked. He coldly informed her that he didn't have time for chit chat. She made several attempts to get an appointment, but he always brushed her off. He was too busy and too important to mess with her.

In less than a year he was diagnosed with Lou Gehrig's disease. Deterioration was rapid, and he was soon confined to a nursing home, unable to move or speak. The nurses were surprised when the young professor came to see him, because he didn't have many visitors. Even family members seldom came. On a table in his room was a stack of his published books and articles, as if to say, "Look what I've done!"

No one cared, and no one came.

Preston Smith grew up on a farm near Lamesa, Texas, worked his way through Texas Tech University, and eventually became Governor of Texas. He had an unusual habit for such a busy and important person: he personally returned every phone call! He never became too busy or too important to return the calls of those who wanted to speak to him. He did it before he became Governor, while he was Governor, and after he left office.

I hope you are not too self-absorbed to show genuine interest in others. Busy? Of course you are. So was Jesus. But he always took time for those who needed him. The position you have achieved may be a gift God has entrusted to you, not just for your own advantage, but also for the benefit of others. Be a faithful steward of that gift. It's sad to see those who have, by God's grace, reached a position where they can help others, but are too self-centered to do it.

Jesus' mission statement clashes with our modern mindset: *"the Son of Man did not come to be served, but to serve ..." (Matthew 20:28).*

Here's Paul's advice:

> *Instead of being motivated by selfish ambition or vanity, each of you should, in humility, be moved to treat one another as more important than yourself. Each of you should be concerned not only about your own interests, but about the interests of others as well (Philippians 2:3-4 NET).*

Don't let these two sentences slip past you: 1) Treat one another as more important than yourself; 2) Be concerned not only about your own interests, but about the interests of others as well.

Eugene Peterson translates Philippians 2:4 this way, *"Forget yourselves long enough to lend a helping hand."*

It would be hard to find a more perfect embodiment of those words than the tiny, stooped, wrinkled woman who was known around the world as Mother Teresa. She became the 20th century icon for compassion, declaring war on human suffering, and stubbornly refusing to surrender.

In 1985, on a flight en route to Mexico City to minister to earthquake victims, Mother Teresa politely asked a flight attendant to find out how much the airline would donate to aid the victims if she skipped the box lunch that had been given her. After inquiring, the attendant quoted a figure of $1. "A dollar it is then," replied the smiling nun. There were 126 passengers and three crew members on board. When word got around, 129 box lunches were returned unopened.

When the plane landed Mother Teresa asked airline administrators for both the $129 *and* the returned lunches—which she received and delivered to Mexico City's homeless.[2]

> *Anything you did for even the least of my people here, you also did for me (Matthew 25:40 NCV).*

What's on your agenda today? Classes? Travel? Work? Meetings? Shopping? Cleaning?

You have it all laid out. But it only takes one phone call to blow those plans to bits. An illness, an accident, a death—even a chatty friend—can rewrite the script. *"... you don't know what the day will bring" (Proverbs 27:1 NLT).*

God's plans may be different from yours. You may have visions of big, headline-worthy accomplishments, while he is planning for your day to be one of small, quiet deeds. The seemingly insignificant may be the most important thing you do today ...

The affirmation of a friend.
The note of encouragement that you write.
The much-longer-than-intended phone conversation.

You may come to the end of the day and write it off as wasted. But God may judge it a smashing success—someone was blessed, and you were the one he used to deliver the blessing.

You Can Make A Difference to One

The first President Bush was fond of telling the story about a man who was walking on the beach with his grandson. The boy picked up each starfish he saw and threw it back into the ocean. "If we leave them here," he said, "they'll die."

"This beach goes on for miles," said his grandfather. "There are thousands of starfish here. What you are doing won't make a difference."

The boy looked at the starfish in his hand, gently threw it into the ocean, and said, "It will make a difference to this one."

You will fill this day with something. How about filling it with something that will make a difference to someone? Both that person and you will be saying …

This is the day the Lord has made;
let us rejoice and be glad in it.

29

TAKE CONTROL

"*Oh!*"

That was her response to every masterpiece of nature. A sunset, a rainbow, a tree, or a flower would bring a gasp from her lips … "*Oh!*"

Awareness is the mother of gratitude, and gratitude the mother of joy.

"*Use your eyes today as if you would be stricken blind tomorrow,*" advised the blind Helen Keller.

"*This is the day the Lord has made!*"

Oh!

Singing in Sorry Circumstances

Andrea, daughter of best-selling author Max Lucado, was five years old at the time, and she was reluctant to give up the day. As Max kissed her goodnight, she lifted heavy eyelids and said, "I can't wait until I wake up."[1]

That's one way of looking at it. Then there's another way, usually an adult way: "I can't wait until this day is over!"

Which is it for you? You have a say in setting the tone of your day, you know.

I will walk cautiously here, because things have happened to some of you that you can't control. Your son is on drugs. Your daughter is getting a divorce. Your husband has lost his job. Your mother has Alzheimer's. With all you have on your plate, how can you be cheerful?

Granted, it's hard to be happy when you're hurting. Still, joy is not entirely at the mercy of circumstance.

Take Paul. Stripped, beaten, and jailed—not in a room-with-a-view, mind you, but in a dark, dirty cell deep in the bowels of the prison. Add cuffs and stocks and you have the picture. Now *that's* a bad day. But in those sorry circumstances, Paul was singing. No kidding, singing![2]

A decade later, when he was under house arrest in Rome, he wrote a letter to his favorite church. A happy letter. The words *rejoice, joy,* and *glad* show up 16 times in it. *"Rejoice in the Lord always,"* he wrote. Then—just in case they missed it—*"I will say it again: Rejoice!" (Philippians 4:4).* His circumstances stunk, but he had learned to be content whatever the circumstances (Philippians 4:11-12).

Molly Picon, star of Yiddish stage and film, spent numberless nights in jam-packed hotel rooms with members of her theatrical company. Grumbling was the common language, but it was a language Molly didn't speak. One night a voice out of the darkness asked her why she, the star, never complained about cramped quarters.

"My grandmother brought up 11 children in four rooms," she answered.

"How did she manage that?" another voice questioned.

"She took in boarders!" Molly answered.

You know people who are always cheerful, even while enduring almost unbearable difficulties. You know the opposite kind of people, too: those who would sulk their way through Disney Land. Chronic complainers. Gruff, grouchy, gloomy, gripey people. People you don't want to be around.

Woody Allen snorted that there are only two kinds of people—the wretched and the miserable. "Thank God if you are only miserable," he growled.

Then there's *Murphy's Law*: "If anything can go wrong, it will."

Woody is wrong! Murphy too!

Can you be cheerful in spite of trouble? Jesus thought so. He said, *"In the world you will have tribulation; but be of good cheer, I have overcome the world" (John 16:33 NKJV).*

To be happy you must …

204

Take Control of Your Attitude

Viktor Frankl was incarcerated in four concentration camps, including the death camp of Auschwitz. His father, mother, brother, wife—everyone in his family except his sister—died in the camps. "Everything," said Frankl, "can be taken from a man but one thing: the last of human freedoms—to choose one's attitude in any given set of circumstances." And William James said, "The greatest discovery of my generation is that human beings can alter their lives by altering their attitudes."

There you go! Take ownership of your attitude. You can't always control circumstances. But you, and only you, can control your attitude.

"Inside of me," said an elderly man, "there are two dogs. One is hostile; one is peaceful. They fight all the time."

"Which dog wins?" he was asked.

"The one I feed the most."

There are two dogs fighting to control your attitude. The one you feed the most will win.

I know a man who consistently feeds the hostile dog and starves the peaceful one. His response to every positive statement is, *"Yeah, but ... "*

"What gorgeous weather!" you say.

"Yeah, but it won't last," he snarls.

"Hear you got a raise."

"Yeah, but insurance and taxes will eat it all up."

He finds a worm in every apple.

Robert Louis Stevenson said, "There is no duty we so much underrate as the duty of being happy." That's quite a statement, coming from a man who spent most of his life as a bedridden invalid. Once, while giving him his medications, his wife said, "Robert, I don't understand how you can be so happy." "My dear," he said, "I am not going to let my disposition be dictated by a row of medicine bottles." He was happy in spite of his illness.

Joy is always "in spite of" something. Karl Barth called joy a "defiant nevertheless." Troubles? Yes! Storms? Of course! *Nevertheless*, you can have a joyful disposition!

On a scale of 1 to 10—1 being very negative and 10 being very positive—how would you grade your attitude? On the same scale how do you think your spouse would grade you? Your best friend? Your co-workers? Your fellow Christians?

Take Control of Your Actions

There is no better way to sweeten your attitude and ramp up your joy than to purposely do something to make someone else happy.

That was one of the requirements of Leo Buscaglia's class on Love at the University of Southern California. Each student had to have a project that served someone's unmet need.

Joel drew a blank—couldn't think of a thing for his project. "What can I do?" he asked.

"Come with me," said Buscaglia.

He took Joel to a nursing home near the university campus; a dismal place. Residents rarely got out of bed and seldom spoke. Just stared at the ceiling. Sick. Lonely. Angry. Afraid.

Joel was puzzled. "What am I suppose to do here?" he asked.

"See that lady over there?" Buscaglia said. "Go over and say hello."

"That's all?"

"That's all."

So Joel went over and said hello.

She looked at him suspiciously, then asked, "Are you a relative?"

He said he wasn't.

"Good!" she replied. "I hate my relatives. Sit down, son."

And they talked ... and talked ... and talked. Joel kept going back to see her. He started visiting other residents too. Soon the day that he made his weekly visit became known as "Joel's Day." The women began having their hair done on "Joel's Day." And dressed in their best.

Dr. Buscaglia was walking across the campus one day when he saw 30 elderly people shuffling down the sidewalk. In front of the group was— you guessed it—Joel, leading his friends to a USC football game. Dr. Buscaglia said that scene was the greatest thrill of his educational career.

And Joel? Well, Joel was about the happiest guy you'd ever hope to see; the most cheerful chap on campus.

Take control of your attitude and actions and you'll be singing this song …

This is the day the Lord has made;
let us rejoice and be glad in it.

30

HAVE A NICE DAY

Carl Honoré was rushing to catch a plane when he spotted a book in the airport gift shop: *One-Minute Bedtime Stories*. Eureka! It seemed like the perfect solution for the nightly ritual with his three-year-old son Benjamin, who always wanted him to read just one more story. He, on the other hand, always wanted to wrap it up, tuck Benjamin in, and retreat to watch TV and answer his email. What could be better than this? Rattle off a half-dozen stories inside ten minutes.

And then he thought, "Have I lost my mind?" Nothing was more important to him than Benjamin. Or shouldn't have been.

Instead of buying the storybook, Honoré wrote a book of his own: *In Praise of Slowness*—an appeal to slow down and enjoy the "now." "A big part of slowing down is doing less," Honoré says.[1]

"Can't do that!" you say.

Bet you can. A review of your schedule is almost certain to reveal chunks of time that are being spent doing things you don't have to do. Americans spend an average of four hours a day watching TV. That's dropping a whopping 28 hours a week into a black hole.

Have a hard look at your *"To Do List."* Anything there that's not all that important? Anything there that someone else should be doing instead of you? Anything there that you could—and probably should—say "no" to?

There is nothing heroic about an overcrowded schedule. We've been sold a bill of goods; duped into believing that a jammed schedule is a sign of importance. The busier you are the more important people think you are, and it bloats your ego. So you run full speed from before dawn until after dark. You're the go-to guy or gal. If it is going to get done, you are the one who has to do it. Everything depends on you. You are indispensable.

Know what? If your name showed up in tomorrow's obituaries, the people and projects that couldn't get along without you would.

Believe it or not, it's not all up to you. Stop trying to cram 14 eggs into a 12-egg carton. Slow down. Take a deep breath. Listen to God's whisper: *"Calm down, and learn that I am God"* (Psalm 46:10 CEV).

I have three "Be Aware" suggestions that will help you put things in perspective, stop the hand-wringing, and bring joy into your life.

Be Aware of the Ordinary Things

Today be intentionally aware of one blessing that you have been taking for granted.

Water, for instance.

Water! Clean water. Running water. Hot water. Cold water. There are many places where running water—to say nothing of hot running water—would be an unimaginable luxury, an out-of-reach blessing. Over 1.2 billion people in our world live without access to safe drinking water.[2]

For this one day refuse to take water for granted. Don't drink a glass of water, or take a shower, or wash a load of clothes, or put dishes in the dishwasher, or water the lawn without being aware of the blessing, and thanking God for it.

When David Steindl-Rast grew up in Nazi-occupied Austria, air raids were a daily experience. One morning when the bombs started falling, David ducked into a nearby church and crawled under a pew to shield himself from flying glass and falling debris. The explosions were ear-splitting and the church was shaking like it was in the grip of a major earthquake. He expected the ceiling to cave in and bury him alive.

After awhile the steady tone of the sirens signaled that the raid was over. Dusting off, David walked out of the church. Buildings that he had trudged past less than an hour ago were now smoking mounds of rubble. Suddenly, in the midst of the wreckage, his eyes fell on a small square of grass. "Never before," he said, "had I seen grass so surprisingly green." He had passed that patch of grass dozens of times without noticing it. But this morning it brought him a moment of awareness that engulfed him in gratitude and joy. It was a glorious May morning.[3]

Don't wait for a storm to jolt you into an awareness of God's grand gifts. Be aware. Be alert. Be grateful. Today notice the ordinary things— the things you usually take for granted. A patch of gorgeous green grass. A flower. A child's smile. Water.

Be Aware of the Things that Count Most

You may have suffered loss. I don't want to make light of that. But I do want to remind you that you may not have lost the most important things: family, friends, health, faith, salvation, and the promises of God.

In the midst of what you lack, be aware of what you have. In the midst of those who have hurt you, be aware of those who love you.

Early Christians experienced harsh words and hard experiences; many had all their possessions confiscated. They didn't just endure such treatment—they accepted it joyfully, because they knew they *"had better and lasting possessions"* (Hebrews 10:32-34).

The prophet Habakkuk saw his nation falling apart. The economy was collapsing, and a war they couldn't win was coming at them. There was part of the prophet that was terrified: his heart was pounding, his lips were quivering, and his legs were trembling (Habakkuk 3:16). But his faith was stronger than his fear. In a burst of trust-rhetoric he vowed, even in the face of disaster, not only to endure, but to rejoice.

> *Though the fig tree does not bud and there are no grapes on the vines, though the olive crop fails and the fields produce no food, though there are no sheep in the pen and no cattle in the stalls, yet I will rejoice in the Lord, I will be joyful in God my Savior (Habakkuk 3:17-18).*

211

That wasn't whistling in the dark, that was God's song in the night. *"Each day the Lord pours his unfailing love upon me, and through each night I sing his songs" (Psalm 42:8 NLT).*

Be Aware of the Things that You Don't Need

Socrates enjoyed strolling through the vendors' stalls in Athens, viewing the plethora of products for sale. "Ah, how many things I have no need of!" he would say.

On an earlier page I mentioned Barry Schwartz's visit to the supermarket, where he found 80 pain relievers, 90 decongestants, 116 skin creams, 360 shampoos, and 150 lipsticks.

That piqued my curiosity and lured me to my corner drugstore, yellow pad in hand. A quick read of labels in the over-the-counter medicines section spilled the beans about the bugs being treated behind my neighbors' closed curtains. Here were rows of remedies for:

> dry eye,
> warts,
> itch,
> athlete's foot,
> hair loss,
> headache,
> backache,
> toothache,
> gum disease,
> heartburn,
> gas,
> cough,
> allergies,
> arthritis,
> insomnia,
> asthma,

flu,
joint stiffness,
overactive bladder,
indigestion,
nausea,
body lice,
ear infection,
strep throat,
ringworm,
shingles,
ulcers,
eczema,
hemorrhoids.

There were more, but that was more than enough.

Back at my desk I experienced a count-your-blessings epiphany! Scrolling down this list of ailments that I don't have, I thanked God that I had no need for the remedies.

How about you? Run your finger down the list. Anything there for which you need no treatment? Yes? So join Socrates' grateful chant: "Ah, how many things I have no need of!"

Joy comes to those who count their blessings. And you don't have to look hard to find a lot to count.

You have a choice in how you treat this day: you can complain ... or you can rejoice and be glad.

Today you can complain about the weather, or you can rejoice and be glad that you have shelter.

Today you can complain about financial strains, or you can rejoice and be glad that you have food and clothes.

Today you can complain because you have to work, or you can rejoice and be glad that you have a job.

Today you can complain about your busy schedule, or you can rejoice and be glad that you are valued and needed.

Today you can complain about aches and pains, or you can rejoice and be glad that you can see, hear, and walk.

Today you can complain about your life, or you can rejoice and be glad that you weren't aborted.

Today is the day to which all of your yesterdays have been pointing since the day of your birth. And the day from which all of your tomorrows will advance until the day of your death. It's the only day there is. All other days have either disappeared into the darkness, or not yet emerged from it. This day is unique. One of a kind. It will be gone before you know it. And it won't be back.

You have been given a limited amount of time. You don't know how much, but you know you've used up a good bit of it. Your calendar is running out of pages.

But you have this page, this day. God made it, and gave it to you to shape.

I hope it will be the best day of your life. Every hour meaningful. Every minute enjoyable.

Have a nice day.

This is the day the Lord has made;
let us rejoice and be glad in it.

Summary Resolutions from Section Six

JOY

This is the day the Lord has made;
let us rejoice and be glad in it.
—Psalm 118:24

I RESOLVE to be alert to some simple pleasure that I have been taking for granted.

I RESOLVE to enjoy my work, doing my job to the best of my ability—with a smile, not a smirk.

I RESOLVE to be kind and thoughtful, regardless of the words or actions of others.

I RESOLVE to do something for someone without expectation of thanks or reward.

I RESOLVE to enjoy *this* day, rather than looking back at the past or forward to the future.

I RESOLVE to be positive and cheerful.

NOTES

Chapter 3: Easter Is Coming

    1. Betty Ford, quoted in Marlo Thomas, *The Right Words at the Right Time* (New York: Attria Books, 2002), 105.

    2. Ibid, 106.

Chapter 4: When You Don't Understand

    1. Adapted from a sermon by Robert Hardies. Original source unknown.

Chapter 5: With You Always

    1. Adapted from F.W. Boreham, *A Bunch of Everlastings* (New York, Cincinnati: The Abingdon Press, 1920), 129-140.

    2. See Matthew 10:16-22; Luke 21:12-16.

Chapter 6: God, Garlic, and Gadgets

    1. See Exodus 15:13; Numbers 11:5.

Chapter 7: The All-Seeing Eye

    1. *Body Worlds* exhibit, The Houston Museum of Natural Science. Thanks to Dr. Ray Jouett for confirming these facts.

Chapter 9: Listen for His Voice

    1. Based on Exodus 3-4.

    2. See Isaiah 45:9; 64:8; Jeremiah 18:4.

3. Luke 5:1-10.
4. John 21:1-12.

Chapter 12: Victory is Just a Decision Away

1. Numbers 14:9.
2. Joshua 1:6, 7, 9.
3. These promises appear in the first nine verses of Joshua 1.
4. John McCain, "In Search of Courage," *Fast Company,* September 2004, 56.
5. Joshua 3.

Chapter 13: Feed Your Faith, Not Your Fear

1. http://www.Phobialist.com
2. Morrie Schwartz, as quoted in Mitch Albom, *Tuesdays with Morrie* (New York: Doubleday, 1997), 118.
3. Ibid.

Chapter 14: Today You Fight ... and Win

1. The comments that follow are based on 1 Samuel 16-26.

Chapter 15: Even There

1. The quotations (in italics) are taken from various translations of Daniel 3:2-27.

Chapter 18: In the Meantime

1. See original story at Luke 1:7-20.
2. Luke 1:14-17.

Chapter 19: I Ought to …

1. Wayne W. Dyer, *Wisdom of the Ages* (New York, NY: Quill, An Imprint of HarperCollins Publishers, 2002), 97.

Section Five Prologue

1. Thornton Wilder, *Our Town* (New York: Perennial Classics, an imprint of HarperCollins, 2003), 97.

Chapter 22: You and Bill Gates

1. William Barclay, *The Gospel of Matthew Volume 1* (Philadelphia: The Westminster Press, 1958), 252.
2. Thornton Wilder, *Our Town* (New York: Perennial Classics, an imprint of HarperCollins, 2003), 87.

Chapter 25: I Know He Watches Me

1. On October 1, 2001, I underwent a successful radical prostatectomy and have been cancer-free ever since.
2. Adapted from John Thomas Oaks, "The Sparrow at Starbucks," *Today's Christian* magazine, November/December 2001, Vol. 39, No. 6, 11.

Chapter 26: Today's Treasures, Tomorrow's Ruins

1. Barry Schwartz, *The Paradox of Choice* (New York, NY: Harper Collins, 2004), 1.
2. Ibid, 9.
3. 2 Chronicles 9:4-12 MSG.

Chapter 27: You're the only You in the World

1. Jeffrey Sonnenfeld and Andrew Ward, *Firing Back, How Great Leaders Rebound After Career Disasters* (Boston, Massachusetts: Harvard Business School Press, 2007), 274.

Chapter 28: You Can Make a Difference

1. Adapted from Jim Wood, http://www.fpcnorfolk.org/sermons.oct312004.htm
2. Ray Simon, *Mischief Marketing* (Chicago, IL: Contemporary Books, 2000).

Chapter 29: Take Control

1. Max Lucado, *And the Angels Were Silent* (Sisters, Oregon: Multnomah Books, 1992), 111.
2. See Acts 16:22-25.

Chapter 30: Have a Nice Day

1. Abridged from Doug Colligan, "Happiness Now." *Reader's Digest,* March, 2005. Pp. 93-99.
2. http://www.betham.org/sermons/sweibacks5762vk.html.
3. David Steindl-Rast, *Gratefulness, the Heart of Prayer* (New York/Mahwah, N.J.: Paulist Press, 1984), 10.

INDIVIDUAL ACTION STEPS
AND
GROUP DISCUSSION GUIDE

FROM THE AUTHOR

John Cheever said, "I can't write without a reader. It's precisely like a kiss—you can't do it alone." Well said! A writer's work is worthless without the reader. You, the reader, are the only one who can make the words of this book worthwhile, by application. This section is designed to help accomplish that. There are two application components for each chapter.

Individual Action Steps
This component is for the individual reader, designed for personal use; six action items to help you reflect on the message and personally apply it. The first three items, and the last, are uniform for each chapter, and are self-explanatory. The fourth and fifth are unique to the message of the chapter being considered.

Group Discussion Guide
This component is for class or group discussion. It assumes that each member of the group has a copy of the book, and has focused on the chapter(s) under discussion previous to the class/group meeting. (If you have a specific number of sessions in which you are required to cover the material, you may need to combine some of the chapters.)

If you have visitors who haven't had opportunity to read the material, it would be worthwhile to read the chapter aloud if time permits. You may wish to assign a member of the class/group to read it; do this a week in advance. Approximate oral reading time is noted at the head of each Discussion Guide session.

The first three questions are common to each chapter. These three questions could take up the entire discussion period, so the group leader will need to gauge the time accordingly, deciding what he/she considers most important to the discussion of each chapter.

The leader is encouraged to keep the group experience positive, supportive, and non-judgmental. Be sensitive to the personal nature of some of the questions, and never try to force participation. Involvement should always be optional.

—Joe Barnett

SECTION ONE
TRUST

Chapter 1: 1628 9th Street

Individual Action Steps

1. Write this *Trust* text on an index card: *Trust in the Lord with all your heart; do not depend on your own understanding (Proverbs 3:5).* Carry it with you and read it often.

2. Write down the main benefit you received from this chapter.

3. Write down what you intend to do as a result.

4. What is the most difficult problem you are presently facing? Read the *Trust* text above and try to apply it to that situation.

5. Re-read the last four paragraphs of the chapter, and make a conscious effort today to be in the right boat with the right person.

6. Before you go to bed tonight rate your level of trust today, on a scale of 1 to 10 (1 being very unsuccessful and 10 being very successful).

GROUP DISCUSSION GUIDE

Approximate oral reading time: 6 minutes.

Present the following comments and questions for class/group discussion:

1. What is the main message you received from this chapter?

2. Did you take any action to make the message personal?

3. What was the result?

4. Do you know of someone who has been through trying circumstances and maintained a high level of trust?

5. Why do you think some are able to trust regardless of the problems that assault them, while others aren't?

6. Peter crumbled and denied Jesus the night of his arrest. Yet, later, when he was facing an almost-certain death sentence, he calmly slept. What do you think brought about this change? Is there a lesson for us here, twenty centuries later?

Chapter 2: A Mixed Bag

Individual Action Steps

1. Continue reading the *Trust* text often: *Trust in the Lord with all your heart; do not depend on your own understanding (Proverbs 3:5).*

2. Write down the main benefit you received from this chapter.

3. Write down what you intend to do as a result.

4. Make a conscious effort today to trust God with no strings attached—to trust him without a "Jacob's List."

5. Today pray this prayer: You are God; I'm not. You know what is best; I don't. I haven't come to you to tell you what to do; I have come to you to ask you to do what is best. I don't know what you will do, but I know it will be the right thing. Amen.

6. Before you go to bed tonight rate your level of trust today, on a scale of 1 to 10 (1 being very unsuccessful and 10 being very successful).

GROUP DISCUSSION GUIDE

Approximate oral reading time: 7 minutes.

Present the following comments and questions for class/group discussion:

1. What is the main message you received from this chapter?

2. Did you take any action to make the message personal?

3. What was the result?

4. Do you ever make demands of God as a prerequisite of trusting him?

5. Have you ever turned a problem over to God, and then reclaimed ownership of it when he didn't handle it the way you wanted him to, or as quickly as you wanted him to?

6. The distraught father said to Jesus, *"I do believe; help me overcome my unbelief!"* What do you think he meant? Is there an application in those words for us?

Chapter 3: Easter Is Coming

Individual Action Steps

1. Continue reading the *Trust* text often: *Trust in the Lord with all your heart; do not depend on your own understanding (Proverbs 3:5).*

2. Write down the main benefit you received from this chapter.

3. Write down what you intend to do as a result.

4. Today apply this double-barreled advice from Betty Ford: 1) If you have committed to something, do it to the best of your ability. 2) If something happens over which you have no control, trust God to guide you.

5. Trust isn't tested when times are easy, but when times are hard. If you are experiencing difficult days see it as a time to exercise your trust muscles.

6. Before you go to bed tonight rate your level of trust today, on a scale of 1 to 10 (1 being very unsuccessful and 10 being very successful).

Group Discussion Guide

Approximate oral reading time: 11 minutes.

Present the following comments and questions for class/group discussion:

1. What is the main message you received from this chapter?

2. Did you take any action to make the message personal?

3. What was the result?

4. The twelve spies who were sent to scout out Canaan had similar backgrounds and experiences. Two of them trusted God; ten of them didn't. Do you see their counterparts among your acquaintances? What causes such different levels of trust?

5. Job's strong statement of trust was, *"Though he slay me, yet will I trust him."* Yet, he struggled with the injustice of his undeserved suffering. Is it possible for us to both question and trust?

6. Compare Israel's wilderness experience, the world of the first-century church, and the world of the twenty-first century church. In which period do you think trust was/is most difficult to achieve?

Chapter 4: When You Don't Understand

Individual Action Steps

1. Continue reading the *Trust* text often: *Trust in the Lord with all your heart; do not depend on your own understanding (Proverbs 3:5).*

2. Write down the main benefit you received from this chapter.

3. Write down what you intend to do as a result.

4. Take a long-range view of trying times, remembering how the ending for Job and Joseph was triumphant, even though the journey had been excruciating.

5. Your understanding is limited; God's isn't. So remember that God knows what he is doing; you may not. He knows where he is taking you; you may not. He knows why; you may not.

6. Before you go to bed tonight rate your level of trust today, on a scale of 1 to 10 (1 being very unsuccessful and 10 being very successful).

Group Discussion Guide

Approximate oral reading time: 12 minutes.

Present the following comments and questions for class/group discussion:

1. What is the main message you received from this chapter?

2. Did you take any action to make the message personal?

3. What was the result?

4. Job's friends' defense of God sounded right and seemed commendable. But their words offended Job and displeased God. What practical lessons can we take away from this?

5. Discuss the statement: "Joseph, Job, and Jesus defined trust by declaring it, not when things were wonderfully good, but when things were terribly bad." Can you share a modern-day example of similar trust?

6. Can you share any insight on how we can maintain trust when painful things happen that we can't understand?

Chapter 5: With You Always

Individual Action Steps

1. Continue reading the *Trust* text often: *Trust in the Lord with all your heart; do not depend on your own understanding (Proverbs 3:5).*

2. Write down the main benefit you received from this chapter.

3. Write down what you intend to do as a result.

4. Jesus said, *"In this world you will have trouble."* He also said, *"I am with you always."* Today consciously trust the second statement as the answer to the first.

5. If you are going through difficult days, remember that what is seen as tragedy today may be seen as triumph when ripened by time, and that the distressing circumstances you are facing in this life may be reclassified as gifts of grace in the next one.

6. Before you go to bed tonight rate your level of trust today, on a scale of 1 to 10 (1 being very unsuccessful and 10 being very successful).

Group Discussion Guide

Approximate oral reading time: 10 minutes.

Present the following comments and questions for class/group discussion:

1. What is the main message you received from this chapter?

2. Did you take any action to make the message personal?

3. What was the result?

4. Discuss these two comments by Corrie ten Boom: 1) "Every experience God gives us is preparation for the future that only he can see." 2) "I wouldn't have chosen the experiences I've had, but I wouldn't take anything for them now." Can you cite an example from your own life, or the life of someone you know, that illustrates those statements?

5. Discuss this statement: "Whether what happens today is good or bad can only be measured by time." As a follow-up to the previous point, can you cite an example from your own life, or the life of someone you know, that illustrates this statement?

6. This ends our discussion of Section One and its theme verse: *"Trust in the Lord with all your heart; do not depend on your own understanding."* How has living with this verse changed you?

    If time permits, discuss the six summary Resolutions at the end of the section.

SECTION TWO

ASSURANCE

Chapter 6: God, Garlic, and Gadgets

Individual Action Steps

1. Write this *Assurance* text on an index card: *He is able to do immeasurably more than all we ask or imagine (Ephesians 3:20).* Carry it with you and read it often.

2. Write down the main benefit you received from this chapter.

3. Write down what you intend to do as a result.

4. You usually see what you expect to see; hear what you expect to hear; feel what you expect to feel. Today make a conscious effort to keep your expectations positive.

5. Today pray this prayer: *In the morning, O Lord, you hear my voice; in the morning I lay my requests before you and wait in expectation (Psalm 5:3).*

6. Before you go to bed tonight rate your level of assurance today, on a scale of 1 to 10 (1 being very unsuccessful and 10 being very successful).

Group Discussion Guide

Approximate oral reading time: 14 minutes.

Present the following comments and questions for class/group discussion:

1. What is the main message you received from this chapter?

2. Did you take any action to make the message personal?

3. What was the result?

4. Discuss the 8 "If you expect ..." items on pages 35-36. What practical steps can you suggest to cultivate positive expectations rather than negative ones?

5. There seems to be a tendency to attribute unanswered prayer to God, but to credit answered prayer to talent, timing, luck, or coincidence. Why?

6. Discuss the statement: "Don't put a period where God puts a comma ... your biography isn't finished yet." Can you cite a time when a seemingly disastrous situation had a happy ending?

Chapter 7: The All-Seeing Eye

Individual Action Steps

1. Continue reading the *Assurance* text often: *He is able to do immeasurably more than all we ask or imagine (Ephesians 3:20).*

2. Write down the main benefit you received from this chapter.

3. Write down what you intend to do as a result.

4. Today make a conscious effort to rely on God's power and count on his presence. Consider these words: *"When you are in trouble, call out to me. I will answer and be there ..." (Psalm 91:15 CEV).*

5. As you go through this day, be aware of the blessings you have received that you didn't ask for.

6. Before you go to bed tonight rate your level of assurance today, on a scale of 1 to 10 (1 being very unsuccessful and 10 being very successful).

Group Discussion Guide

Approximate oral reading time: 11 minutes.

Present the following comments and questions for class/group discussion:

1. What is the main message you received from this chapter?

2. Did you take any action to make the message personal?

3. What was the result?

4. Discuss Bagger Vance's comment: "Ain't a soul in this entire earth ain't got a burden to carry that he can't understand. You ain't alone in that, but you have been carrying this one long enough. It's time to lay it down." Can you give some practical pointers on how we can lay aside the problems, anxieties, grudges, anger, etc. that we have been carrying far too long?

5. Name some of the blessings we have received that we haven't specifically asked for. How can we become more aware and more thankful?

6. Do you ever hit dry patches in your prayer life? Do you have suggestions on how to jump-start a sluggish prayer life?

Chapter 8: The Hardest Prayer to Pray

Individual Action Steps

1. Continue reading the *Assurance* text often: *He is able to do immeasurably more than all we ask or imagine (Ephesians 3:20).*

2. Write down the main benefit you received from this chapter.

3. Write down what you intend to do as a result.

4. Today when you pray put God's will first and your requests second.

5. Be aware that God often receives conflicting requests: a "Yes" answer to your prayer might require a "No" answer to the prayer of one of his other children. Resolve to be satisfied with the answer he gives.

6. Before you go to bed tonight rate your level of assurance today, on a scale of 1 to 10 (1 being very unsuccessful and 10 being very successful).

Group Discussion Guide

Approximate oral reading time: 9 minutes.

Present the following comments and questions for class/group discussion:

1. What is the main message you received from this chapter?

2. Did you take any action to make the message personal?

3. What was the result?

4. Re-read and discuss the first four paragraphs of this chapter. Can you give some suggestions on how we can resolve the mentioned conflicts that crowd God out of our lives?

5. Instead of praying "Your will be done," we usually pray for what *we* want to be done, and ask God to use his power to make it happen. Do you agree with that statement? If so, can you make some suggestions on how to reverse it?

6. Discuss this verse: *"If we ask anything according to his will he hears us" (1 John 5:14).* What does it mean?

Chapter 9: Listen for His Voice

Individual Action Steps

1. Continue reading the *Assurance* text often: *He is able to do immeasurably more than all we ask or imagine (Ephesians 3:20).*

2. Write down the main benefit you received from this chapter.

3. Write down what you intend to do as a result.

4. Meditate on this verse today: *"The Lord himself goes before you and will be with you; he will never leave you nor forsake you. Do not be afraid; do not be discouraged" (Deuteronomy 31:8).*

5. Think of one thing you think God wants you to do differently; one thing that you think he wants you to change. And do it.

6. Before you go to bed tonight rate your level of assurance today, on a scale of 1 to 10 (1 being very unsuccessful and 10 being very successful).

Group Discussion Guide

Approximate oral reading time: 11 minutes.

Present the following comments and questions for class/group discussion:

1. What is the main message you received from this chapter?

2. Did you take any action to make the message personal?

3. What was the result?

4. God chose people whose names we know well: Abraham, Moses, Mary, Paul. And those whose names are obscure: Andronicus, Urbanus, Apelles, Persis. Each was chosen to do what God wanted him/her to do. Do you believe that God has also chosen each of us for specific assignments? And equipped us for them?

5. Discuss Dr. Niebuhr's prayer:

    God, give us Grace to accept with Serenity the things that cannot be changed.

    Courage to change the things that should be changed,

    And Wisdom to distinguish the one from the other.

6. Do you have suggestions about how to keep our faith intact and our attitude positive when things don't work out the way we hoped they would?

Chapter 10: God's "More"

Individual Action Steps

1. Continue reading the *Assurance* text often: *He is able to do immeasurably more than all we ask or imagine (Ephesians 3:20).*

2. Write down the main benefit you received from this chapter.

3. Write down what you intend to do as a result.

4. When God gives you something different from what you ask for, don't see it as rejection, but as an add-on to your request.

5. If it seems that God says "No" to your prayer, keep an eye out for his "More."

6. Before you go to bed tonight rate your level of assurance today, on a scale of 1 to 10 (1 being very unsuccessful and 10 being very successful).

Group Discussion Guide

Approximate oral reading time: 10 minutes.

Present the following comments and questions for class/group discussion:

1. What is the main message you received from this chapter?

2. Did you take any action to make the message personal?

3. What was the result?

4. Discuss the opening story of this chapter, about Sue and Baby Robby. Can you relate a similar story, where seeming tragedy turned out to be a blessing?

5. Talk about a time when God gave you "more" than you asked for—a generous add-on to your request.

6. Now talk about a time when God's "more" was something totally different from what you asked for.

   If time permits, discuss the six summary Resolutions at the end of the section.

SECTION THREE
COURAGE

Chapter 11: An Inside Job

Individual Action Steps

1. Write this *Courage* text on an index card: *Be strong and courageous! Do not be afraid or discouraged. For the Lord your God is with you wherever you go (Joshua 1:9 NLT).* Carry it with you and read it often.

2. Write down the main benefit you received from this chapter.

3. Write down what you intend to do as a result.

4. Beginning today let the words *never* and *always* describe you: *never* complain, *always* smile.

5. Today refuse to let anyone control your attitude. Regardless of circumstances or people that have caused you pain, take ownership of your own attitude.

6. Before you go to bed tonight rate your level of courage today, on a scale of 1 to 10 (1 being very unsuccessful and 10 being very successful).

Group Discussion Guide

Approximate oral reading time: 9 minutes.

Present the following comments and questions for class/group discussion:

1. What is the main message you received from this chapter?

2. Did you take any action to make the message personal?

3. What was the result?

4. Discuss the "faces of courage" on page 73. Can you relate real-life stories that illustrate those statements? What other life-circumstances could be in that list?

5. Discuss the statement: "What sets courageous people apart is that they refuse to give up." Can you cite some examples?

6. Consider these words from this chapter: "Someone hurt your feelings. Broke your heart. Shattered your dreams. Let it go! Move on. Forgive. However badly someone has treated you, and however deeply it hurts, get over it." Is that really possible? Do you know someone who has done it? Can you offer some counsel on how to accomplish it?

Chapter 12: Victory is Just a Decision Away

Individual Action Steps

1. Continue reading the *Courage* text often: *Be strong and courageous! Do not be afraid or discouraged. For the Lord your God is with you wherever you go (Joshua 1:9 NLT).*

2. Write down the main benefit you received from this chapter.

3. Write down what you intend to do as a result.

4. You can't have a happy future if you are hanging on to a painful past. Decide today that you will release your hold on the past.

5. Ask God for wisdom to focus on the future, and for courage to take the first positive step into it.

6. Before you go to bed tonight rate your level of courage today, on a scale of 1 to 10 (1 being very unsuccessful and 10 being very successful).

Group Discussion Guide

Approximate oral reading time: 11 minutes.

Present the following comments and questions for class/group discussion:

1. What is the main message you received from this chapter?

2. Did you take any action to make the message personal?

3. What was the result?

4. Is someone in your family, or a close friend, facing a "comparison crisis"—being compared to a highly successful family member, peer, or predecessor? How do you help such a person maintain a healthy self-image?

5. Talk about the difficulty of transitioning into unfamiliar territory: new town, new job, new challenge. Or living in difficult circumstances due to divorce, death, etc. If you have been through such changes, how did you negotiate them and survive?

6. Can you give some suggestions on how to give up the past and focus on the future?

Chapter 13: Feed Your Faith, Not Your Fear

Individual Action Steps

1. Continue reading the *Courage* text often: *Be strong and courageous! Do not be afraid or discouraged. For the Lord your God is with you wherever you go (Joshua 1:9 NLT).*

2. Write down the main benefit you received from this chapter.

3. Write down what you intend to do as a result.

4. Give thought to these words today: *"We are perplexed because we don't know why things happen as they do, but we don't give up and quit ... We get knocked down, but we get up again and keep going" (2 Corinthians 4:8-9).*

5. And here is another verse to consider: *"Do not fear, for I am with you; do not be dismayed, for I am your God. I will strengthen you and help you; I will uphold you ..." (Isaiah 41:10).*

6. Before you go to bed tonight rate your level of courage today, on a scale of 1 to 10 (1 being very unsuccessful and 10 being very successful).

Group Discussion Guide

Approximate oral reading time: 15 minutes.

Present the following comments and questions for class/group discussion:

1. What is the main message you received from this chapter?

2. Did you take any action to make the message personal?

3. What was the result?

4. Read and discuss the parable in Luke 12:13-21. In our materialistic, consumer-oriented society, how do we keep from measuring our worth by our possessions?

5. Comparing your success or failure to the success or failure of others is almost certain to result in either pride or despair. In a competitive society how do we avoid such comparisons?

6. Discuss the following: "You can't sweep up the trash of past mistakes anymore than you can unscramble an egg. So you messed up. Knowing what you know now, you would do a better job if you had another shot at it. But you didn't know then what you know now, and you don't have another shot at it. So stop looking in the rearview mirror. You have zero control over the past."

Chapter 14: Today You Fight ... and Win

Individual Action Steps

1. Continue reading the *Courage* text often: *Be strong and courageous! Do not be afraid or discouraged. For the Lord your God is with you wherever you go (Joshua 1:9 NLT).*

2. Write down the main benefit you received from this chapter.

3. Write down what you intend to do as a result.

4. Today—by written note, phone call, or face-to-face—give a word of encouragement to someone you know who is discouraged.

5. And while you're at it, resolve that you will not make a discouraging or negative comment to anyone today.

6. Before you go to bed tonight rate your level of courage today, on a scale of 1 to 10 (1 being very unsuccessful and 10 being very successful).

Group Discussion Guide

Approximate oral reading time: 12 minutes.

Present the following comments and questions for class/group discussion:

1. What is the main message you received from this chapter?

2. Did you take any action to make the message personal?

3. What was the result?

4. Everyone faces the disabling giant of discouragement at some point. Can you offer some practical pointers on how to defeat it?

5. When a dominant personality—parent or spouse, for example—attempts to dictate a direction that is contrary to a person's interests and desires, how should one respond?

6. And how should one respond to repeated put-downs?

Chapter 15: Even There

Individual Action Steps

1. Continue reading the *Courage* text often: *Be strong and courageous! Do not be afraid or discouraged. For the Lord your God is with you wherever you go (Joshua 1:9 NLT).*

2. Write down the main benefit you received from this chapter.

3. Write down what you intend to do as a result.

4. Today share the theme verse (#1 above) with someone you know who is going through a difficult time.

5. Be consciously aware that you are not alone. God's companionship is *wherever* and *forever.*

6. Before you go to bed tonight rate your level of courage today, on a scale of 1 to 10 (1 being very unsuccessful and 10 being very successful).

Group Discussion Guide

Approximate oral reading time: 11 minutes.

Present the following comments and questions for class/group discussion:

1. What is the main message you received from this chapter?

2. Did you take any action to make the message personal?

3. What was the result?

4. It took enormous courage for Shadrach, Meschach, and Abednego to stand by their convictions in a hostile environment. Can you cite examples of this level of conviction and courage in our go-along-to-get-along age?

5. Do Christians worry less, fear less, and get discouraged less than non-Christians?

6. This chapter affirms that firm faith in the presence of God is the source of strength and courage, and the key to elimination of fear and discouragement. How would you define "firm faith in the presence of God?"

   If time permits, discuss the six summary Resolutions at the end of the section.

SECTION FOUR
PATIENCE

Chapter 16: The Waiting Room

Individual Action Steps

1. Write this *Patience* text on an index card: *Wait for the Lord; be strong and take heart and wait for the Lord.* Carry it with you and read it often.

2. Write down the main benefit you received from this chapter.

3. Write down what you intend to do as a result.

4. Today make a personal application of these words to whatever difficulty you face: Jesus *"spoke to them and said, 'Take courage! It is I. Don't be afraid.' Then he climbed into the boat with them, and the wind died down"* (Mark 6:50-51).

5. When it seems that God moves slowly, remind yourself that he has his reasons, and resolve to let him set the pace.

6. Before you go to bed tonight rate your level of patience today, on a scale of 1 to 10 (1 being very unsuccessful and 10 being very successful).

Group Discussion Guide

Approximate oral reading time: 12 minutes.

Present the following comments and questions for class/group discussion:

1. What is the main message you received from this chapter?

2. Did you take any action to make the message personal?

3. What was the result?

4. Why do you think Jesus waited so long to come to his disciples when they were caught in the storm? Why do you think he sometimes delays his coming to us when we face tough times?

5. Charles Swindoll said, "The most difficult discipline in the Christian life, in my opinion, is waiting." Do you agree? Disagree? Why?

6. Waiting can be agonizing. This can be especially true when it relates to job loss, health issues, etc. Can you give an example of where the wait resulted in a more favorable result than a quick answer would have?

Chapter 17: Anything but That!

Individual Action Steps

1. Continue reading the *Patience* text often: *Wait for the Lord; be strong and take heart and wait for the Lord.*

2. Write down the main benefit you received from this chapter.

3. Write down what you intend to do as a result.

4. In this hurry-up age we tend to cram every minute with "productive" activity. Today take three ten-minute breaks to pray.

5. Take time to think about these words: *"I wait quietly before God, for my hope is in him" (Psalm 62:5 NLT).*

6. Before you go to bed tonight rate your level of patience today, on a scale of 1 to 10 (1 being very unsuccessful and 10 being very successful).

Group Discussion Guide

Approximate oral reading time: 14 minutes.

Present the following comments and questions for class/group discussion:

1. What is the main message you received from this chapter?

2. Did you take any action to make the message personal?

3. What was the result?

4. Technology has changed the way we live and work. How have these changes impacted relationships?

5. Are you more or less patient today than you were ten years ago? What has caused the change?

6. Which of the "wait verses" cited at the end of the chapter is most meaningful to you? Why?

Chapter 18: In the Meantime

Individual Action Steps

1. Continue reading the *Patience* text often: *Wait for the Lord; be strong and take heart and wait for the Lord.*

2. Write down the main benefit you received from this chapter.

3. Write down what you intend to do as a result.

4. Waiting is hard. But God's timing is always perfect. Today be mindful that God is waiting on you to learn to wait on him.

5. Today pray this prayer: Dear God, I ask you to give me grace to wait patiently until it pleases you to answer my prayer. For I believe you will do it in your own time and in your own way. Amen.

6. Before you go to bed tonight rate your level of patience today, on a scale of 1 to 10 (1 being very unsuccessful and 10 being very successful).

Group Discussion Guide

Approximate oral reading time: 11 minutes.

Present the following comments and questions for class/group discussion:

1. What is the main message you received from this chapter?

2. Did you take any action to make the message personal?

3. What was the result?

4. Zechariah's prayer was eventually answered. But it was so long coming that he had given up hope. Has that ever happened to you?

5. Discuss Paul's words in 2 Corinthians 4: *"We are perplexed because we don't know why things happen as they do, but we don't give up and quit ... We get knocked down, but we get up again and keep going ... we never give up" (2 Corinthians 4:8-9, 16 TLB)*. Do you know someone who exemplifies those words?

6. Discuss this statement: "It pleases us when God is quick to answer; it pleases him when we trust him even when he delays. It is human to want to see before believing; it is Spirit-led to believe before seeing." Can you give some practical pointers on how to develop that level of patience?

Chapter 19: I Ought to ...

Individual Action Steps

1. Continue reading the *Patience* text often: *Wait for the Lord; be strong and take heart and wait for the Lord.*

2. Write down the main benefit you received from this chapter.

3. Write down what you intend to do as a result.

4. Choose one item from the "I ought to" list and consciously act on it today.

5. Choose a second item from the "I ought to" list—this time one that is a bit more difficult to tackle. Resolve to make a beginning. The suggestions on page 132 may be helpful.

6. Before you go to bed tonight rate your level of patience today, on a scale of 1 to 10 (1 being very unsuccessful and 10 being very successful).

Group Discussion Guide

Approximate oral reading time: 11 minutes.

Present the following comments and questions for class/group discussion:

1. What is the main message you received from this chapter?

2. Did you take any action to make the message personal?

3. What was the result?

4. Did you find anything in the "I ought to" list that pinpointed a need in your life? Did you act on it? If you are comfortable doing so, will you share the result with the group?

5. Some of the "oughts" in the list call for attitude control. Others require action. Which do you find the most difficult?

6. This chapter asserts that one of the main reasons we fail to change destructive attitudes, alter bad behavior, or repair damaged relationships is because we don't make the beginning. A few action-starter suggestions are made. Can you give additional ideas on how we can jump-start action?

Chapter 20: The Race of Your Life

Individual Action Steps

1. Continue reading the *Patience* text often: *Wait for the Lord; be strong and take heart and wait for the Lord.*

2. Write down the main benefit you received from this chapter.

3. Write down what you intend to do as a result.

4. Determine that you will not permit impatience to spoil a single moment of your life today.

5. Focus on one area of your life where you need to exercise more patience, and start working on it today.

6. Before you go to bed tonight rate your level of patience today, on a scale of 1 to 10 (1 being very unsuccessful and 10 being very successful).

Group Discussion Guide

Approximate oral reading time: 11 minutes.

Present the following comments and questions for class/group discussion:

1. What is the main message you received from this chapter?

2. Did you take any action to make the message personal?

3. What was the result?

4. Impatience often causes us to act foolishly. And it wrecks relationships. Can you think of an occasion where patience rescued a situation from an unhappy ending?

5. "If at first you don't succeed, forget it!" seems to be a prevalent attitude in our impatient world. We are tempted to give up too quickly. Can you share an event or project from your life, or the life of someone you know, where patient refusal to give up paid rich dividends?

6. Living an exemplary Christian life is not always easy. Discuss these words from Hebrews: *"Let us run with patience the race that is set before us" (Hebrews 12:1 ASV)*. Expand the discussion by reading the entire paragraph—Hebrews 12:1-3.

   If time permits, discuss the six summary Resolutions at the end of the section.

SECTION FIVE
PEACE

Chapter 21: Let Him Carry Your Stuff

Individual Action Steps

1. Write this *Peace* text on an index card: *Let him have all your worries and cares, for he is always thinking about you and watching everything that concerns you (1 Peter 5:7 TLB).* Carry it with you and read it often.

2. Write down the main benefit you received from this chapter.

3. Write down what you intend to do as a result.

4. Today be the person who shares the burdens of others; be the person who is concerned about the concerns of others. Be conscious of those who need you, and carry their stuff.

5. Pray Anne Lamott's brief but comprehensive prayer today: *"Help me, help me, help me. Thank you, thank you, thank you."*

6. Before you go to bed tonight rate your level of peace today, on a scale of 1 to 10 (1 being very unsuccessful and 10 being very successful).

Group Discussion Guide

Approximate oral reading time: 9 minutes.

Present the following comments and questions for class/group discussion:

1. What is the main message you received from this chapter?

2. Did you take any action to make the message personal?

3. What was the result?

4. Discuss the following statement from this chapter: "God wants to take on your worries and cares. Little ones and big ones; trivial ones and tragic ones. None is too small to escape his concern, and none too large for him to handle." He may want to use you to administer his concern. How can we be more sensitive to the worries and cares of others? Can what seems trivial to you be a matter of crushing concern to someone else?

5. Discuss these words from Paul: *"Do not be anxious about anything, but in everything, by prayer and petition, with thanksgiving, present your requests to God. And the peace of God, which transcends all understanding, will guard your hearts and your minds in Christ Jesus"* (Philippians 4:6-7).

6. This chapter asserts that it is difficult (some say impossible) to worry and be thankful at the same time. Do you agree? Disagree?

Chapter 22: You and Bill Gates

Individual Action Steps

1. Continue reading the *Peace* text often: *Let him have all your worries and cares, for he is always thinking about you and watching everything that concerns you (1 Peter 5:7 TLB).*

2. Write down the main benefit you received from this chapter.

3. Write down what you intend to do as a result.

4. Today focus on Jesus' words: *"Can any of you by worrying add a single hour to your span of life?" (Matthew 6:27 NRSV).*

5. Turn the tables on Satan today by refusing to judge anyone's worth by his/her wealth, but by their value in God's sight.

6. Before you go to bed tonight rate your level of peace today, on a scale of 1 to 10 (1 being very unsuccessful and 10 being very successful).

Group Discussion Guide

Approximate oral reading time: 12 minutes.

Present the following comments and questions for class/group discussion:

1. What is the main message you received from this chapter?

2. Did you take any action to make the message personal?

3. What was the result?

4. We live in a time and place that emphasizes material success and judges a person's worth by where he lives, what she drives, and the wealth he/she has accumulated. The New Testament censures such appraisal (see James 2:1-4). How can we avoid judging by the standards of the society in which we live?

5. As a follow-up to the previous point, isn't it true that our own self-image is largely linked to our material success or failure? Do you have some suggestions about how to deal with this?

6. Discuss William Barclay's comment: "Surely there is no better description of a man's god, than to say that his god is the power in whom he trusts; and when a man puts his trust in material things, then material things have become, not his support, but his god."

Chapter 23: You Don't Have to Shout

Individual Action Steps

1. Continue reading the *Peace* text often: *Let him have all your worries and cares, for he is always thinking about you and watching everything that concerns you (1 Peter 5:7 TLB).*

2. Write down the main benefit you received from this chapter.

3. Write down what you intend to do as a result.

4. Is there a family member or friend that you have neglected too long? Today write a note or make a phone call to that person. Affirm your gratitude for the relationship and apologize for being so busy with other matters that you haven't given it the attention it deserves.

5. Today stop whatever you are doing long enough to perform a random act of kindness. Make a special effort to give attention to someone you frequently see but usually ignore. (Hint: waitress, janitor, fellow-employee, fellow-student.)

6. Before you go to bed tonight rate your level of peace today, on a scale of 1 to 10 (1 being very unsuccessful and 10 being very successful).

Group Discussion Guide

Approximate oral reading time: 11 minutes.

Present the following comments and questions for class/group discussion:

1. What is the main message you received from this chapter?

2. Did you take any action to make the message personal?

3. What was the result?

4. If you followed the suggestions in #4 and/or #5 in the "Individual Action Steps" above, would you share the result of one of those actions with us?

5. Discuss this comment: "I don't remember a single one of those important things that cluttered my calendar that day. But I vividly remember that girl sitting on the curb crying." Can you give some suggestions on how we can show more concern for the feelings and needs of those we encounter when we are faced with a crowded calendar?

6. You have probably seen a wrist-band or pendant with the letters WWJD: *What would Jesus do?* Discuss some situations we frequently face in our encounters with people, and apply that question.

Chapter 24: I Choose Peace

Individual Action Steps

1. Continue reading the *Peace* text often: *Let him have all your worries and cares, for he is always thinking about you and watching everything that concerns you (1 Peter 5:7 TLB).*

2. Write down the main benefit you received from this chapter.

3. Write down what you intend to do as a result.

4. Today be an instrument of peace, using the prayer of Francis of Assisi as a guide:

   Lord,
   Make me an instrument of thy peace.
   Where there is hatred, let me sow love;
   Where there is injury, pardon;
   Where there is doubt, faith;
   Where there is despair, hope;
   Where there is darkness, light;
   Where there is sadness, joy.

   O divine Master,
   Grant that I may not so much seek
   To be consoled as to console,
   To be understood as to understand,
   To be loved as to love;
   For it is in giving that we receive;
   It is in pardoning that we are pardoned;
   It is in dying to self that we are born to eternal life.

5. Take control of your attitude by use of these two sentences: *I have the right to choose. I choose peace.*

6. Before you go to bed tonight rate your level of peace today, on a scale of 1 to 10 (1 being very unsuccessful and 10 being very successful).

Group Discussion Guide

Approximate oral reading time: 14 minutes.

Present the following comments and questions for class/group discussion:

1. What is the main message you received from this chapter?

2. Did you take any action to make the message personal?

3. What was the result?

4. We often seek peace of mind in the wrong places. Review the three "wrong places" mentioned on page 166. Can you think of other "wrong places" we turn to in search of peace?

5. Peace of mind is an inside job. It is not events that determine our level of peace, but how we react to those events. Do you have some suggestions on how we can control our reactions to unpleasant events?

6. As a follow-up to the previous point discuss the final section of this chapter which centers on these two sentences: *I have the right to choose. I choose peace.*

Chapter 25: I Know He Watches Me

Individual Action Steps

1. Continue reading the *Peace* text often: *Let him have all your worries and cares, for he is always thinking about you and watching everything that concerns you (1 Peter 5:7 TLB).*

2. Write down the main benefit you received from this chapter.

3. Write down what you intend to do as a result.

4. Keep this thought in the forefront of your thinking today: Whatever concerns you, concerns God. He is *"watching everything that concerns you."*

5. As a follow-up to the previous point, give thought today to the lyrics of *His Eye is on the Sparrow:*

   > *I sing because I'm happy;*
   > *I sing because I'm free.*
   > *For His eye is on the sparrow*
   > *And I know He watches me.*

6. Before you go to bed tonight rate your level of peace today, on a scale of 1 to 10 (1 being very unsuccessful and 10 being very successful).

Group Discussion Guide

Approximate oral reading time: 9 minutes.

Present the following comments and questions for class/group discussion:

1. What is the main message you received from this chapter?

2. Did you take any action to make the message personal?

3. What was the result?

4. David wrote: *"When I look at the night sky and see the work of your fingers—the moon and the stars you have set in place—what are mortals that you should think of us, mere humans that you should care for us?" (Psalm 8:3-4 NLT).* What are your thoughts on this mind-boggling scripture?

5. Have you ever seen a dead bird and thought that God was aware of its death? Consider these words of Jesus: *"Not even a sparrow, worth only half a penny, can fall to the ground without your Father knowing it. ... So don't be afraid; you are more valuable to him than a whole flock of sparrows" (Matthew 10:29, 31 NLT).* Talk about what that means to you.

6. The theme verse for this section is 1 Peter 5:7. A familiar translation reads: *"Cast all your anxiety on him because he cares for you."* In our development of these chapters we have used THE LIVING BIBLE translation: *"Let him have all your worries and cares, for he is always thinking about you and watching everything that concerns you."* Discuss the promises that you are always in his thoughts and never out of his view.

    If time permits, discuss the six summary Resolutions at the end of the section.

SECTION SIX

JOY

Chapter 26: Today's Treasures, Tomorrow's Ruins

Individual Action Steps

1. Write this *Joy* text on an index card: *This is the day the Lord has made; let us rejoice and be glad in it (Psalm 118:24).* Carry it with you and read it often.

2. Write down the main benefit you received from this chapter.

3. Write down what you intend to do as a result.

4. As you move about today, be aware of everything you see—buildings, houses, shops, restaurants, etc.—and remind yourself that these are all future ruins. Then spend some time contemplating these words: *"So we fix our eyes not on what is seen, but on what is unseen. For what is seen is temporary, but what is unseen is eternal" (2 Corinthians 4:18).*

5. Today make a list of the five things in your life for which you are most grateful, and lay them before God in a prayer of thanksgiving.

6. Before you go to bed tonight rate your level of joy today, on a scale of 1 to 10 (1 being very unsuccessful and 10 being very successful).

Group Discussion Guide

Approximate oral reading time: 9 minutes.

Present the following comments and questions for class/group discussion:

1. What is the main message you received from this chapter?

2. Did you take any action to make the message personal?

3. What was the result?

4. Can you think of a time when you thought life would hardly be worth living unless you could have a certain possession? How important is that possession to you today?

5. Read and discuss Ecclesiastes 2:4-11, and Ecclesiastes 2:17-23.

6. Discuss this statement: "Outer circumstances are temporary. Whether you're a dishwasher or head honcho, it's a temporary job. Whether you live in a shack or a mansion, it's temporary housing. If your happiness is tied to the temporary you are terribly vulnerable." You probably agree with that statement in principle, but can you give some suggestions on how we can pull it off living in a materialistic society?

Chapter 27: You're the only You in the World

Individual Action Steps

1. Continue reading the *Joy* text often: *This is the day the Lord has made; let us rejoice and be glad in it (Psalm 118:24).*

2. Write down the main benefit you received from this chapter.

3. Write down what you intend to do as a result.

4. "There is no one else in the world like you. Never has been. Never will be. You are an original. One-of-a-kind. You're the only *you* in the world. That's who God made you. And he didn't make a mistake." Spend some time today contemplating that statement, and celebrating your individuality.

5. Paul told Timothy, *"Do not neglect your gift ..."* (*1 Timothy 4:14*). Today read Romans 12:6-8. See if you can find your gift there, and resolve that you will use it, not neglect it.

6. Before you go to bed tonight rate your level of joy today, on a scale of 1 to 10 (1 being very unsuccessful and 10 being very successful).

Group Discussion Guide

Approximate oral reading time: 13 minutes.

Present the following comments and questions for class/group discussion:

1. What is the main message you received from this chapter?

2. Did you take any action to make the message personal?

3. What was the result?

4. Remember Paul Orfalea's advice? *"Work with your strengths, not your weaknesses. If you're not good at something, do something else. Go where you are strong."* Do you think parents sometimes push their children to pursue careers they are unsuited for, or that don't match their interests? As parents—or grandparents—how can we encourage our children or grandchildren to reach high, while being sensitive to their interests and abilities?

5. Paul said that *"Christ has given each of us special abilities—whatever he wants us to have out of his rich storehouse of gifts"* *(Ephesians 4:7 TLB)*. Read and discuss Romans 12:6-8. As you consider members of this group, can you see in them specific gifts mentioned in this passage? It would be appropriate to give affirmation to them by thanking them for using their gift well.

6. Discuss this statement: "Being happy is making peace with who you are and with what you can do—and refusing to beat up on yourself for who you aren't and for what you can't do."

Chapter 28: You Can Make a Difference

Individual Action Steps

1. Continue reading the *Joy* text often: *This is the day the Lord has made; let us rejoice and be glad in it (Psalm 118:24).*

2. Write down the main benefit you received from this chapter.

3. Write down what you intend to do as a result.

4. Today invest five minutes in prayer for someone you know who is hurting.

5. Bring joy to a relative or friend by writing a note of affirmation.

6. Before you go to bed tonight rate your level of joy today, on a scale of 1 to 10 (1 being very unsuccessful and 10 being very successful).

Group Discussion Guide

Approximate oral reading time: 12 minutes.

Present the following comments and questions for class/group discussion:

1. What is the main message you received from this chapter?

2. Did you take any action to make the message personal?

3. What was the result?

4. Do you have a prayer list? Is it a written list, or a mental one? How do you determine whose name is on your list? How often do you pray for them? Do you tell them that you are praying for them?

5. Read and discuss Philippians 2:3-4. Can you offer some practical suggestions on how we can fulfill the demands of these words?

6. Discuss this statement: "The seemingly insignificant may be the most important thing you do today ... The affirmation of a friend. The note of encouragement that you write. The much-longer-than-intended phone conversation." How do you deal with interruptions? With frustration? Seeing them as an annoying intrusion? Seeing them as a door God is opening? Operating on a crowded schedule, how do you decide what is important and what is insignificant?

Chapter 29: Take Control

Individual Action Steps

1. Continue reading the *Joy* text often: *This is the day the Lord has made; let us rejoice and be glad in it (Psalm 118:24).*

2. Write down the main benefit you received from this chapter.

3. Write down what you intend to do as a result.

4. Be intentionally aware of the beauty around you today. The blind Helen Keller said, "Use your eyes today as if you would be stricken blind tomorrow."

5. Today get creative: purposely do something to make someone happy.

6. Before you go to bed tonight rate your level of joy today, on a scale of 1 to 10 (1 being very unsuccessful and 10 being very successful).

Group Discussion Guide

Approximate oral reading time: 9 minutes.

Present the following comments and questions for class/group discussion:

1. What is the main message you received from this chapter?

2. Did you take any action to make the message personal?

3. What was the result?

4. Paul was under house arrest when he wrote these words: *"I have learned to be content whatever the circumstances. I know what it is to be in need, and I know what it is to have plenty. I have learned the secret of being content in any and every situation, whether well fed or hungry, whether living in plenty or in want" (Philippians 4:11-12).* How do you think he was able to develop such a positive attitude under such negative circumstances? Do you have some suggestions on how we can achieve that kind of attitude?

5. Robert Louis Stevenson, who spent most of his life as a bedridden invalid, said, "I am not going to let my disposition be dictated by a row of medicine bottles." Can you tell us about someone you know who has maintained a sunny disposition in spite of being ill? What is the secret of their joy?

6. Remember Joel's story in this chapter? Is there something we could do as a group to bring meaning and joy to some people? A nursing home, assisted-living facility, or retirement center project? A hospital activity? Something else?

Chapter 30: Have A Nice Day

Individual Action Steps

1. Continue reading the *Joy* text often: *This is the day the Lord has made; let us rejoice and be glad in it (Psalm 118:24).*

2. Write down the main benefit you received from this chapter.

3. Write down what you intend to do as a result.

4. Today don't drink a glass of water, take a shower, wash clothes, wash dishes, or water the lawn without being aware of the taken-for-granted blessing of water, and thanking God for it.

5. Joy comes to those who count their blessings. Today make a list of 10 things for which you are grateful.

6. Before you go to bed tonight rate your level of joy today, on a scale of 1 to 10 (1 being very unsuccessful and 10 being very successful).

Group Discussion Guide

Approximate oral reading time: 12 minutes.

Present the following comments and questions for class/group discussion:

1. What is the main message you received from this chapter?

2. Did you take any action to make the message personal?

3. What was the result?

4. In this chapter we are urged to be aware of ordinary things. Can you think of some ordinary taken-for-granted blessings that we should be more aware of, and more thankful for?

5. Our theme verse in this section has been: *"This is the day the Lord has made; let us rejoice and be glad in it."* Do you have thoughts to share on what this verse now means to you?

7. We have reached the end of this study. Will you share with the group the major benefit you have received from our discussions?

   If time permits, discuss the six summary Resolutions at the end of the section.

CPSIA information can be obtained at www.ICGtesting.com
Printed in the USA
BVOW020314180612

292930BV00002B/2/P